Getting Started
with Literature Circles

Getting Started with Literature Circles

Katherine L. Schlick Noe, *Seattle University*
Nancy J. Johnson, *Western Washington University*

Christopher-Gordon Publishers, Inc.
Norwood, Massachusetts

Credits

Every effort has been made to contact copyright holders for permission to reproduce borrowed material where necessary. We apologize for any oversights and will be happy to rectify them in future printings.

Photographs used with permission of teachers and students.
Student work used with permission.

The Bill Harp Professional Teacher's Library
An Imprint of
Christopher-Gordon Publishers, Inc.
1502 Providence Highway, Suite 12
Norwood, MA 02062
(800) 934-8322

Printed in the United States of America

10 9 8 7 6 5 4 3 2   05 04 03 02 01 00 99

ISBN: 0-926842-97-8

Contents

Acknowledgments vii

Introduction ix

Chapter 1 Building a Framework for Literature Circles 1

Where Do Literature Circles Fit into Everything Else I'm Teaching? 1
What Benefits Will My Students Attain? 2
How Do I Set Goals That Will Get Me Started? 3
How Do I Teach to Reach the Goals I've Set? 4
Some Final Thoughts on Setting Goals 5

Chapter 2 Classroom Climate 7

Establish a Climate of Collaboration and Respect 7
Establish a Climate of Independence and Responsibility 8
Establish a Climate of Response 9
Some Final Thoughts on Classroom Climate 10
Common Questions About Climate 10

Chapter 3 Structure 11

What Do Literature Circles in Different Classrooms Have in Common? .. 11
Planning a Timeline 11
Putting the Pieces Together 14
A Glimpse into Two Classrooms 22
Vicki Yousoofian, First Grade 22
Lori Scobie, Fourth Grade 27
Some Final Thoughts on Structure 32
Common Questions About Structure 32

Chapter 4 Good Books for Literature Circles 35

What Makes a Good Literature Circle Book? 35
What Books Do I Start With? 36
How Do I Find Books to Fit a Range of Reading Abilities and Interests? 38
How Do I Obtain Multiple Copies? 38
What Are Some Good Book Sets to Use? 38
Some Final Thoughts on Good Books 40
A Question About Books 40

Chapter 5 Discussion 41

What Are Your Goals for Discussion? 42
Selecting a Discussion Format 43
A Discussion Framework 43

Assessing and Evaluating Discussions 56
Some Final Thoughts on Discussion 59
Common Questions About Discussion 59

Chapter 6 Response Journals 63

Clarify Your Purposes for Response Journals 64
Help Students Understand the Purpose of Response Journals 65
Help Students Understand How to Focus Their Journal Responses 65
How and Why Response Journals Change Over Time 71
Teaching the Response Forms 72
Assessing and Evaluating Journal Responses 74
Some Final Thoughts on Response Journals 76
Common Questions About Response Journals 76

Chapter 7 Focus Lessons: Incorporating Literacy Strategies 81

What Are Focus Lessons? Why Do Them? 81
Where Do Focus Lessons Come From? 82
Types of Focus Lessons 82
Components of a Focus Lesson 86
Keeping Track of Focus Lessons 87
Some Final Thoughts on Focus Lessons 88
Common Questions About Focus Lessons 89

Chapter 8 Extension Projects 91

Definitions and Benefits 91
Extension Project Possibilities 92
Extension Project Focus 93
The Process of Extension Projects 94
Guiding Students Through the Process 95
Extension Project Presentations 101
Assessing and Evaluating Extension Projects 102
Some Final Thoughts on Extension Projects 103
Common Questions About Extension Projects 105

Final Thoughts 107

References 109

Children's Literature Cited 111

Index 113

Acknowledgments

This book would not have come to life without the teachers and students who welcomed us to observe, support, and learn from their first experiences with literature circles. We are indebted to those teachers: Adam Brauch, Kristin Gerhold, Janine A. King, Mary Lou Laprade, Lori Scobie, and Vicki Yousoofian. We are equally grateful to the students in grades 1-6 who graciously allowed us to use their words, photographs or samples of their work to illustrate this book: Kate Bakamis, Sally Bogus, Jennifer Borland, Jamie Renee Brown, Marc Browning, Annie Christie, Elise Contreras, Brett Eisenhart, Conor Fitzgerald, Symphony Hayes, Patrick Hinds, Derek Holt, Krista Hoy, Brad Jauron, Jeremy Kraner, Valerie Lamb, Caitlin Larsen, Sally Latimer, Kate McWilliams, Jarrett Moore, Mobi Njoku, Jack Noe, Andrew Peek, Leslie Phillips, Max Pollard, Reed Roy-Byrne, Nick Shaker, Morgan Vane, Josef Vonderau, and Olga Zuyeva. Additionally, we extend our thanks to colleagues who have contributed their ideas, experiences, and thoughtful reviews: Patti Castelli, Elizabeth Fuller, Kristin Garis, Kristen Gephart, Chris Gustafson, Gail Huizinga, Sue Johnson, Gordon Kelly, Dan Kryszak, Connie LaTendresse, Linda Lee, Rhonda Cox Mased, Betty Murrell, Ruthanne Parker, and Judy Riegel. Finally, we deeply appreciate the loving support and faith of our families: Russell, Joseph, and Jack Noe; and Fred Bannister.

Introduction

If any of the following descriptions fits, this book is for you:

- You've heard about literature circles and they sound intriguing. You may already be in an adult book group and know how talking about books with other readers sometimes makes all the difference in what you get out of a book. You may already know that discussion strengthens students' ability and motivation to read. Perhaps you have a colleague who uses literature circles, you've read about them, or you've heard them described in a workshop.
- You've jumped in and tried literature circles, but what erupted in your classroom is a long way from your vision of meaningful, focused discussion and profound insights into literature.
- Or, you've taken a few successful first steps and are ready for some guidance that will take you to the next level.

What Are Literature Circles?

Let's define what we mean by "literature circles." Although you may know them by other names—literature study groups, book clubs, discussion circles—these terms describe teaching approaches with common elements. In literature circles, small groups of students gather together to discuss a piece of literature in depth. The discussion is guided by students' response to what they have read. You may hear talk about events and characters in the book, the author's craft, or personal experiences related to the story. Literature circles provide a way for students to engage in critical thinking and reflection as they read, discuss, and respond to books. Collaboration is at the heart of this approach. Students reshape and add onto their understanding as they construct meaning with other readers. Finally, literature circles guide students to deeper understanding of what they read through structured discussion and extended written and artistic response.[1]

As described in this book, literature circles take many forms and engage students in meaningful response to literature in a variety of ways. Every teacher you will meet here has a slightly different image of literature circles in his or her classroom. Perhaps the easiest way to understand what literature circles *are* is to also look at what they *are not* (Figure I.1).

Student choice, responsibility, and personal response are key elements. The paradox is this: Although decidedly student centered, literature circles only work when the

---

[1]For excellent discussions of the research base for literature circles, we recommend the following resources: Sarah Owens' chapter, "Treasures in the Attic: Building the Foundation for Literature Circles," in *Literature Circles and Response*; Dixie Lee Spiegel's article in the October 1998 issue of *The Reading Teacher*: "Silver Bullets, Babies, and Bath Water: Literature Response Groups in a Balanced Literacy Program"; *Peer Talk in the Classroom: Learning from Research,* edited by Jeanne Paratore and Rachel McCormack; and *Research and Professional Resources in Children's Literature,* edited by Kathy Short.

Literature Circles are . . .	Literature Circles are not . . .
• Reader response centered • A component of a balanced literacy program • Groups of readers formed by book choice • Structured for student independence, responsibility, and ownership • Guided primarily by student insights and questions • Intended as a context in which to *apply* reading and writing skills • Flexible and fluid; never look the same twice	• Teacher and text centered • The entire reading curriculum • Teacher-assigned groups formed solely by ability • Unstructured, uncontrolled "talk time" without accountability • Guided primarily by teacher- or curriculum-based questions • Intended as a place to do skills work • Tied to a prescriptive "recipe"

Figure I.1 Literature Circles *Are . . .* and *Are Not . . .*

teacher provides effective structure and scaffolding. Too little structure is one of the reasons literature circles fail—and the reason some teachers abandon them. On the other hand, organizing too tightly can inhibit students' motivation and ownership. Learning to walk that thin line—and discovering what works for you and your students—is what this book is about.

Underlying Assumptions

How you conceptualize your teaching, relate to your students, and prepare for literature circles will have a direct impact on how well they work in your classroom. Therefore, we offer the following assumptions that underlie successful literature circles:

- **My students can learn to love reading *and* become stronger readers and writers through literature circles.**   Marie Clay defines reading as "a message-gaining, problem-solving activity which increases in power and flexibility the more it is practiced" (1991, p. 6). In literature circles, students collaborate with others to gain the message and solve problems in reading. In the process, they become more motivated readers. Third grade teacher Mary Lou Laprade put it this way: "I think (literature circles) make kids want to read. They just think joining a book club is such hot stuff. They want to read on their own, and they want to read books that other kids have talked about. Literature circles give them plenty of practice doing it—reading together and talking about books."

- **My classroom is a safe, respectful, and productive place in which everyone's view counts.**   Everyone needs to feel safe in order to share deeply-held feelings, argue with an author, or express a view that goes against a conversation's drift. Literature circles must provide that safety, and teachers need to lay the foundation of respect and productivity. This key element of classroom climate needs to be nurtured from the first few days of school. As first grade teacher Vicki Yousoofian said, "We talk about the importance of being caring people, and how we need to do that throughout our classroom and with our friends and family. We're creating that kind of a climate—and it is very apparent in the literature circle groups."

- **My students can build the structure with me.**   You do not have to have all of the answers if you invite students to help you. For many teachers, this can be a big relief. Lori Scobie talked through problems with her fourth graders: "I had them tell me what wasn't working and had them help me think of what we were going to do to fix it. I wasn't play acting—I really wanted to know." Lori explains the value of including her students in decision making this way: "I don't have to sit down and think it all up. I can ask 28 other people for help. Even though they're a third my age, they always come up with better stuff."

The main message that we hope you receive is this: There are as many "right" ways to organize and implement literature circles as there are teachers and students eager to begin them. If your question is, "Is it OK to . . .?" or "Can I . . .?", the answer is "Yes." If your question is, "Do I have to . . .?", the answer is "No."

We hope that you find this book to be *descriptive*, not *prescriptive*. We want to give you a boost to begin, offer some insights from other teachers who may be one or two steps ahead of you, and help you clarify where to go next. This is a book to help you get started.[2]

How This Book Is Organized

Literature circles must fit your beliefs about teaching and learning in order for them to work in your classroom. Therefore, we begin with a framework for literature circles—what you want for your students and for yourself as you begin. Next, we give an overview of how teachers structure literature circles at varying grade levels, from first through sixth. Each component—choosing books, reading and gathering information, discussion, written response, focus lessons, extension projects—is then covered in more depth in a separate chapter.

Each chapter concludes with "What is worth worrying about and what is worth letting go?" and answers to some common questions that teachers ask.

Key Questions

This book attempts to answer some of the burning questions that stand in the way of getting started (or persevering) with literature circles. You may prefer to read straight through the book to build the "big picture" for yourself. Or you may want to start with your most pressing questions and read those chapters. Figure I.2 shows where you will find answers to the questions we hear over and over as we visit classrooms and talk with teachers.

Meet Our Collaborators

This book would not exist without the collaboration of the teachers and students who invited us into their classrooms to share in their first steps with literature circles. We'd like you to meet them—you will visit these classrooms throughout the book. We worked with three teachers during their first year of teaching: Adam Brauch and his third graders at Fairmount Elementary and Kirstin Gerhold and her fifth graders at Columbia Elementary in Mukilteo, Washington; and Lori Scobie and her fourth graders at North City Elementary in Shoreline, Washington. We are also grateful to three teachers, all veterans, who were new to literature circles: Janine King and her sixth graders and

---

[2] When you're ready for more in-depth work in literature circles, we urge you to consider the range of helpful resources available, among them *Literature Circles and Response,* edited by Bonnie Campbell Hill, Nancy J. Johnson, and Katherine L. Schlick Noe; *Literature Study Circles in a Multicultural Classroom,* by Katharine Davies Samway and Gail Whang; and *Literature Circles: Voice and Choice in the Student-Centered Classroom,* by Harvey Daniels.

Vicki Yousoofian and her first graders at St. Joseph's School in Seattle; and Mary Lou Laprade and her second/third graders at John Hay Elementary in Seattle.

If your question is . . .	You'll find answers in . . .
What are literature circles and why should I do them? Where do they fit with the rest of my literacy program? What goals can I meet through literature circles?	Ch. 1 Goals (and Introduction)
How do I build in student ownership, responsibility, and independence?	Ch. 2 Climate (and all chapters)
When and how do I start? What's the first thing I do? How long will each literature circle set last? How many literature circles should I plan in a year? How many groups should I have? How do I form groups? How do I make sure the groups are workable *and* as many students as possible get their first choice?	Ch. 3 Structure
How many discussions a week? How much time should a discussion take? Do kids have to have roles? What about noise level?	Ch. 3 Structure (and Ch. 5 Discussion)
What about my students who can't read well?	Ch. 3 Structure (and Ch. 7 Focus Lessons)
What books work best for literature circles? How do I get enough books? How can I find out about good book lists to use?	Ch. 4 Selecting Books
How do I help students prepare for discussions? How can we develop discussion guidelines together? What should I look for (and help students look for) in their discussions? How can I record my observations? What should I expect from their discussions? How can I continue to foster quality discussions?	Ch. 5 Discussion
What do journals look like? What do students write about? Do students use journals in their discussions? How? How do I respond to all the entries? How many entries do students write a week? How do I get more than one-sentence responses?	Ch. 6 Response Journals
Where can I get a list of focus lesson topics I might want to teach? How will I know if they're comprehending if I'm not asking questions?	Ch. 7 Focus Lessons
How is an extension project different from a book report? Should extensions involve the whole group or should students do them individually? How do I help students plan their projects? How can I make sure students continue to revisit the book through their extension projects?	Ch. 8 Extension Projects

Figure I.2 Finding Answers to Your Questions

CHAPTER 1

Building a Framework
for Literature Circles

... I'll continue to give students the conditions they need to fine tune and orchestrate: lots of time to write and read, freedom to make choices, and chances to talk with others about the choices they make. This is the bedrock on which my beliefs about literacy learning and teaching are founded. Beyond it, I'm not sure what any of us will do next. And this is the sheer joy of it.

I will be surprised every day I teach.

—Nancie Atwell, *In the Middle* (1987, p. 255)

Literature circles, like any aspect of teaching, work best when they "fit" our students, our teaching context, our beliefs, and our own teaching lives. In thinking about where literature circles belong in your classroom and how they might work most effectively, we suggest that you consider these questions:

- Where do literature circles fit into everything else I'm teaching?

- What benefits will my students attain?

- How do I set goals that will help me get started?

- How do I teach to reach the goals I've set?

While we can't answer these questions for you, we can offer possibilities. We do this by focusing on the thinking and decision making of a few teachers who recently included literature circles in their literacy programs. You may find their experiences provide shape and support for the way you frame your literature circles questions. In doing so, we hope you'll also clarify your beliefs, your goals, and your rationale for the why, where, and how of literature circles in your classroom.

Where Do Literature Circles Fit
into Everything Else I'm Teaching?

Setting goals and making plans for literature circles may become more manageable when you consider where and how they fit within your entire literacy program. Literature circles are most successful when they're not expected to *be* the literacy program. Their value comes from the opportunities they provide readers and writers to *apply* literacy skills and strategies learned through other components of the literacy curriculum.

Notice how literature circles fit within the framework of other reading and writing experiences (Figure 1.1). A balanced literacy program—including a place for the explicit teaching of skills and strategies (shared and guided reading and writing) and time for implicit learning (read aloud and independent reading and writing)—provides the ideal

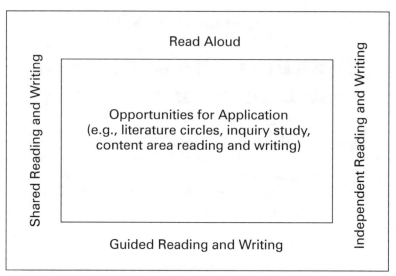

Figure 1.1 Framework for Literature Circles

context for literature circles and authentic opportunities for application.

Providing an extensive definition of each component listed in this literacy program frame—along with teaching suggestions for each—is beyond the scope of this book. If you're interested in more in-depth information about the components of a balanced literacy program, we recommend the following resources: *Reconsidering a Balanced Approach to Reading* (Weaver, 1998); *Balanced Literacy Instruction* (Au, Carroll, & Scheu, 1997); *Guided Reading: Good First Teaching for All Students* (Fountas & Pinnell, 1996); and *Invitations: Changing as Teachers and Learners K-12* (Routman, 1991, 1994).

What Benefits Will My Students Attain?

Your reasons for trying literature circles began to take shape before you opened this book. Perhaps you've selected literature circles because you're aware there are many benefits to be acquired from them. Choosing literature circles is a professional decision with benefits you can plan for, as well as those that occur in the magical encounters sparked by readers and books.

One of the biggest benefits from literature circles is the opportunity they offer readers to meet and talk about commonly read books. When readers discuss insights, raise questions, cite related experiences, wonder about or puzzle over situations prompted by what they read, literature takes on a new life. Interpretation is dynamic. But it's limited when we read alone. When we provide our students—regardless of age or ability—a place to discuss their own interpretation and listen to other readers add *their* interpretation, a book becomes even more meaningful. Literature circles involvement benefits *all* readers because it acknowledges the ideas, experiences, and interpretations of readers as they grow in their understanding of what they read.

A related benefit from literature circles is the active involvement students have as readers. Rather than passively waiting for others to impose questions and assign worksheets, students commit to reading because *they* raise the questions and *they* consider their own experiences as they respond through talk, writing, drama, and art. Their starting points as readers and their continued work through the literature requires activity, not activity sheets. It demands thinking and it takes shape because of the transaction between readers *and* the literature (Rosenblatt, 1978).

The benefits you discover from literature circles will certainly be more inclusive than extended interpretation and active involvement. They'll grow from the goals you set and the experiences, both serendipitous and planned, you and your students encounter.

How Do I Set Goals That Will Get Me Started?

Begin with goals that seem most reasonable and manageable. When you set such goals— whether very general or specifically focused on one component of literature circles—you begin the process of planning your teaching. This process works most naturally when it begins with the goal, then moves through decisions of how to teach, what to demonstrate, and ways to involve students in the plans. You might begin by asking three basic questions:

- What's my goal for this round of literature circles?
- Why is this an important goal?
- How can I teach to this goal?

When setting a goal for your first few literature circles experiences, it's important to have something in mind, otherwise every aspect of literature circles may overwhelm you. We suggest two possible strategies: Start simply and let your goals grow as you do, or set a goal based on one component.

Start Simply and Let Your Goals Grow with You

First grade teacher Vicki Yousoofian's very first literature circles goal was "just to do it, to just try it." After experiencing a full year teaching with literature circles, Vicki refined her goals:

> Now my goals would be for students to develop their love of reading, helping them make the connection between reading and writing, and developing their thinking abilities, their thinking process skills. It would also be to orally communicate about books using the vocabulary that goes with it.

Vicki's second-year goals were influenced by experience, knowledge of and confidence in her first graders' abilities to participate in literature circles, and her growing sense of what makes for richer literary involvement. During her third year, Vicki's goals and related teaching plans continued to take shape:

> My students have to look more deeply in the literature. They have to make connections, personal connections. . . . I think that when we pull out the skills or we ask them questions about the story, we're the ones leading the instruction. If I ask them what they think, what they see, they actually have to think about it and they have to look into the literature and make references from that.

Making personal connections as readers and supporting ideas and opinions with evidence from the story became Vicki's focus. Both goals are concrete and teachable, but neither was an area Vicki could see as important until she started simply, with an initial goal of "just doing it"!

Set a Goal Based on One Component of Literature Circles

Kirstin Gerhold's goal for her fifth graders' first literature circle experience was specific and focused:

> I wanted to teach my students how to discuss a book, and I wanted the first literature circle experience not to be a long, tedious process. So, I thought we should start with a short book, then we'll learn how to talk, and then we'll sort of go from there.

As a result of this desire to work on one key component of literature circles, Kirstin guided her students in the process of discussing and provided tools to support them. In doing so, she needed to stop worrying about whether her students were doing the best they could with other literature circle components. Once Kirstin's students gained competence and confidence with discussions, she could re-set her goals and focus on another component. Until then, she had to keep her sanity by focusing specifically on one component at a time.

How Do I Teach to Reach the Goals I've Set?

Once you set a goal that addresses your students' needs and takes into consideration your specific teaching situation, it's time to plan what and how you'll teach. The remaining chapters in this book provide specific ideas about how to do this. Many also include teaching examples presented in focus lessons. Before stepping into those, we suggest taking a look at one teacher's thinking as she set goals and initiated the planning for using literature circles in her classroom for the first time.

One Teacher's Goal Setting and Planning

Like most teachers new to literature circles, fourth grade teacher Lori Scobie's plan took shape as the year progressed. In Chapter 3, Figure 3.14 shows you how Lori's first year of literature circles evolved. To see how this works, let's walk through some of Lori's goals and planning decisions as she thought about the number and kind of literature circle cycles she wanted that year. We will focus briefly on these decisions in this section, and elaborate with more details in later chapters.

It's easy to feel overwhelmed. When we implement new curricular plans, it's often difficult to know what we're doing in one week, let alone for the entire year. Before you toss this book aside, knowing it'd be impossible for you to make similar plans, realize this: While it appears that Lori developed an ambitious schedule of literature circles during her first year, in reality, the schedule developed itself. Lori didn't lay out her entire year at one time. In September, Lori began thinking through her first literature circle cycle, which she planned to begin the next month. Figure 1.2 shows as much of the calendar as she could envision at that time.

Month	Book Selections & Topic/Theme/Genre	Teaching/ Learning Focus	Books Chosen Because . . .
September		Developing a classroom climate in preparation for literature circles	

Figure 1.2 Literature Circles Calendar: Lori Scobie's Initial Plans

September's focus was on developing a classroom climate to support the work of literature circles. (For more about climate, see Chapter 2.) When Lori started planning in September, she didn't know exactly what her first literature circle cycle would be, and she didn't discover the key ingredient—a full class set of one book—until the end of October. The focus for her first cycle was determined by the set of books she found in the library, *Dear Mr. Henshaw* (Cleary, 1983). October came and went. When November arrived, and literature circle work finally started, Lori didn't realize that her students would still be working with *Dear Mr. Henshaw* in January!

During Lori's first year, her calendar evolved. She knew that she wanted eventually to explore a substantive theme through literature circles. She also knew that she and her students needed time to experience literature circles and learn the processes before this could take place. What she couldn't foresee was how it would all come together.

You will probably discover the same thing. With each round of literature circles, you and your students will learn more about what you're doing and how you want to do things. Most of the teachers we've worked with had that experience their first year. By the second and third years, you will probably find that you can set a more detailed calendar early—and actually stick with it. You will also alter your schedule from year to year to accommodate variations in your literacy program and other teaching needs.

Such decision making demands some initial plans and trusting their evolution. A look at how Lori moved from creating a climate conducive to literature circles (September and October) to learning the structure of literature circles (November–February) to refining the structure through a thematic and genre focus (March through May), gives us a window into her thinking. It started when she made the professional decision to include literature circles as part of her literacy curriculum. It continued when she set some manageable goals and made decisions that moved the goals from her head onto paper and into her classroom. You'll see how Lori's teaching/learning decisions affect the structure of literature circles in her classroom even more clearly when you read Chapter 3.

Some Final Thoughts on Setting Goals

In *On Learning to Read: A Child's Fascination with Meaning*, Bruno Bettelheim and Karen Zelan make this claim: "If we wish to open the world of literacy to our children, what they are asked to read should from the very beginning help them to understand themselves and their world" (1981, p. 306). Literature circles emphasize reading as a creative process and the resulting benefits have the potential to help children better understand themselves as readers. For many of us, that's a goal we hold most dear and one upon which we base our teaching.

We're aware there are many ways to teach to a goal. We're also aware that too many ideas can become overwhelming, even paralyzing. When you're feeling this way, be sure to read "What is Worth Worrying About" and "What is Worth Letting Go" at the end of each chapter, as well as the commonly asked questions. While we can't anticipate every one of *your* questions, we can share questions, experiences, and teaching examples from other teachers, trusting these to support you as you get started setting goals and teaching to reach them.

The benefits that you discover from literature circles may include specific literacy-related skills, such as the ability to support ideas by citing evidence from the text. They may also include benefits that extend beyond literacy, such as collaborating or learning to negotiate, even when it's difficult. Remember, the benefits you discover are influenced by the elements that frame your literacy program as well as the goals you set for your particular group of students at specific points in the year.

What is worth worrying about?

- Remember that literature circles aren't *the* literacy program; rather, they're an application of literacy skill and strategy.

- Selecting one goal or focus helps maintain your ability to remain sane and effective as you plan for literature circles.

- Realize you have time (even in a school year) to focus on more than one goal.

- Accept that neither you nor your students will be good at every aspect of literature circles immediately.

- Give yourself permission to work on the same goal throughout the year.

What is worth letting go?

- Concern that you haven't included everything that's important for literacy development.

- The need to work on every goal you initially set at the beginning of the year.

- Feelings of failure when your students' conversations, responses, and involvement don't look or sound like the examples in this book or in the classroom next door.

- The need to delay beginning until you know exactly how you'll reach your goals.

CHAPTER 2

Classroom Climate

We cultivate an atmosphere of caring and respect from the first day of school. This is one of the most important elements of successful learning—and successful literature circles. One of our first tasks as a class is to generate a large chart listing qualities of caring that we will live by in Room 1B. This chart hangs prominently in the front of the room and we refer to it daily.

—Vicki Yousoofian, first grade teacher

Successful literature circles depend on a classroom climate in which everyone feels valued. Without underlying expectations about the kind of atmosphere you will encourage in your classroom, literature circles cannot flourish. Cultivating a nourishing climate for literature circles involves attention to the following:

- Collaboration and respect
- Independence and responsibility
- Response to literature

Establish a Climate of Collaboration and Respect

When Lori Scobie began her first year of teaching, she knew that she wanted her fourth grade classroom to be a place where everyone had a voice. She had some ideas on how to get there, but an inclusive climate evolved over time as she and her students got to know each other. For her, one of the most important reasons to establish such a climate was to make it possible for everyone to participate in—and benefit from—literature circles. This was particularly important in Lori's classroom because of the children who walked through her door. Many struggled with reading—and even with learning English. Lori noticed that students for whom reading came easily often showed little patience with those who found it frustrating.

Lori realized early in the year that her ESL and Title 1 students needed additional support in order to read the books for literature circles. But would that mean they couldn't participate? She said, "If I were to do guided reading with them while the rest were doing literature circles—that wouldn't be fair to them. It was the social interactions, being able to participate with a book that maybe they never would have been able to read on their own, that made it important for them to take part in the literature circles." To achieve this goal, Lori had to help all students see that everyone—regardless of their ability—could contribute to the literature circle.

7

Here is what Lori recommends you do to establish an inclusive climate from the first day of school:

- **Make clear what you value.**   Articulate to your students that your classroom is one that values diversity and respects differences of opinion.

- **Infuse collaboration throughout the day.**   Form different groups for various purposes across subject areas. Keep groups heterogeneous and flexible. Teach students how to make decisions and solve problems as part of a team.

- **Introduce skills of respectful interaction.**   Help students learn how to talk with one another productively in many classroom settings from class meetings to social studies. Brainstorm, practice, and post a list of ways to "respectfully disagree" and to introduce a point of view. Teach students tools to help them carry on a conversation. Chapter 5 offers specific strategies to teach discussion etiquette and other components of collaboration within literature circle discussions.

With clear expectations—and the skills to enact them—Lori found that her students began to accept one another and function collaboratively in their literature circles. Students began to listen more attentively to each other, participated in supportive partner reading with classmates who struggled, and grew into a community of learners.

Establish a Climate of
Independence and Responsibility

Literature circles offer an ideal context in which to build students' independence and sense of responsibility—not just to you, but to themselves and their classmates. As Janine King says, her sixth graders learn that "The ball is in your court now and you're going to have to make these decisions and you're going to be responsible for them." When they're in a classroom where they do that in all aspects of their learning, such as coming up with their own class rules, it's a natural transition to literature circles.

Mary Lou Laprade knows her third graders' needs well:

> Kids need to know the parameters. We need to help them be independent. When I'm working with the book club, I can't have kids asking, "Where's the paper? Where's a pencil? Can't I go to the bathroom? I can't read this word." They have to know how to do things. So I start the year teaching them how to write journals so they're not just sitting there looking at the page because they don't know how to spell a word. If they need a piece of paper or a pencil, they know where to get it. If they're finished doing whatever they're supposed to do, they know what else they can do. They can go get a book and read. But they know that ahead of time.

Skills of independence need to be nurtured throughout the year in all aspects of the classroom. There are numerous ways that teachers build these skills, knowing that increased independence will pay off in a more satisfying literature circle experience for everyone.

Teach Skills for Independence

With her third graders, Mary Lou Laprade starts slowly, introducing new independence skills every few weeks. "I teach them 'This is journal writing and here's how you do it.' They learn how to do all of the things that later I'll expect them to do on their own while I'm with a book club. They don't have to have my help directly."

Before the literature circles begin in the morning, Mary Lou and her class review the question: "What is it you need to do today?" She posts directions on the board (Figure 2.1). The list includes any unfinished work students need to complete as well as the day's assignments. When students have questions, Mary Lou teaches them to ask someone at their table or to look around the room and see what other students are doing. The result of these efforts, says Mary Lou is this: "Children want this, I think. They want to be busy. They want to do interesting, meaningful, relevant things. And they've got a lot of good ideas. So you teach them—and you give them that freedom to be independent thinkers and to be responsible."

Mary Lou is typical of many teachers who prize literature circles as a part of their curriculum: "I put a high value on independence and I expect kids to become independent. I set it up so that they know what I'm expecting them to do. And I think that frees them a lot, too."

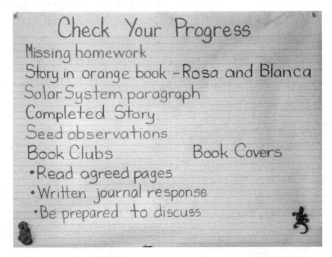

Figure 2.1
Reading Workshop
Directions

Establish a Climate of Response

A third component of classroom climate is response to literature. Are various forms of response infused throughout the literacy curriculum? If so, students will find it much easier to apply these principles to literature circles.

Model Response Through Daily Read Aloud

A simple way to build a climate of response is to begin with your daily read-aloud book. Capitalize on students' natural inclination to talk, wonder, and raise questions. For a few minutes after each read aloud, model your own response and invite students to share their thoughts on what is happening in the book. This doesn't need to take a lot of time, but it builds students' understanding of response that can carry over to their literature circle discussions and writing. If you close the book and say, "OK, time for math," you've lost an opportunity to thread response throughout your students' day.

Watch for Unanticipated Opportunities to Model Response

Lori Scobie took every chance she could find to draw students' attention to examples of response. Sometimes the moment came when she read aloud or when a student made a comment about something the class was studying. Lori would stop, and say, "Did you hear that? Mobi just gave us an example of the language he noticed in *Satchmo's Blues*. That's the kind of writing authors use to paint pictures for us." When noticing author craft or explicitly making personal connections to literature becomes a deliberate part of your teaching, students grow in their understanding of a wide range of responses that they can later try out in literature circles.

Some Final Thoughts on Classroom Climate

Setting a positive climate early in the year—before you begin your first literature circle—gives your students some key strategies for success. Ralph Peterson and Maryann Eeds identified the foundation for an effective classroom climate when they said, "Trust the books, trust the students, and trust yourself" (1991, p. 125). Most of all, trust yourself to guide your students—then get out of their way.

What is worth worrying about?

- Take the time to think through the atmosphere you want to build in your classroom.

- Focus on climate from the first day of school.

- Invite your students to take responsibility for the ways in which everyone is treated—then teach specific ways to show respect, collaborate, and disagree.

What is worth letting go?

- Fear of how students will respond to your expectations for collaboration and independence. When students feel that they have a valued role in building the climate for literature circles—and when they learn the skills to do so—they'll thrive. It may take time but it is well worth the effort on everyone's part.

Common Questions About Climate

I'm ready to start literature circles <u>now</u> and it's already March—how can I go backward to build a climate of collaboration at this point?

    The most important thing is to keep your expectations reasonable. Work off of the strengths you observe in how your students interact with one another. Focus on what works well. Maybe *this* year with *this* class you won't do full-blown literature circles. Perhaps you'll use your read-aloud book to work on simple discussion strategies whereby you can maintain a sense of control and keep students focused on learning to interact one step at a time. Chapter 5 suggests some good starting points. Use your experiences now to plan for next year. We highly recommend Kary Brown's chapter in *Literature Circles and Response*, "Going With the Flow: Getting Back on Course When Literature Circles Flounder" (1995) for concrete and useful ways to get through any rough spots.

CHAPTER 3

Structure

Pick one thing and begin. Even if you have a book and the kids get together and talk about it, and you never have them write—just so you've done <u>something</u>. You can always build from where you start.

—Kirstin Gerhold, fifth grade teacher

Structuring literature circles to work most effectively in your classroom can be a challenge. You'll need to make many decisions, such as how students will choose books, how you will form groups, and how many groups will meet at a time. It can be overwhelming. But take Kirstin Gerhold's advice: "Pick one thing and begin."

In this chapter, we present "getting started" guidelines for structuring literature circles. We'll show you possible variations for each of the following decisions:

- Planning a timeline: Setting a year's calendar and weekly and daily schedules
- Choosing books and forming groups
- Setting up the discussion format
- Incorporating written and extended response
- Managing the structure

Each chapter that follows goes into more detail about the various components of structure introduced here.

What Do Literature Circles in Different Classrooms Have in Common?

Regardless of the grade level you teach or the experiences you and your students have had, literature circles share many common elements. For example, Figure 3.1 shows how three teachers at different grade levels structured their first literature circles. Before we examine each component of the structure more specifically, take a look at the similarities and differences across the three classrooms.

Each teacher made decisions according to her knowledge of herself, her students, and her instructional needs. Therefore, it is important to note that differences in how these teachers structured their literature circles are *not* related solely to grade level. Other teachers at the same grade levels would, of course, make different decisions—as will you. But this is where Vicki Yousoofian, Lori Scobie, and Janine King began.

Planning a Timeline

First, a nod toward reality: Most teachers we know were not able to do much advanced planning when they first started literature circles. For the most part, they just plunged

Teacher/Grade Level	V. Yousoofian 1st	L. Scobie 4th	J. King 6th
Choosing Books	Teacher gives book talk Ballot Teacher forms groups	Teacher gives book talk Ballot Teacher forms groups	Teacher gives book talk Ballot Teacher forms groups
Time Frame	1 week	3–4 weeks	4–6 weeks
Schedule	Teacher sets discussion schedule Students read one book/story a week One group meets at a time with teacher Groups meet once during the week	Teacher sets discussion schedule Groups meet one to two times weekly for discussion or other activity All groups meet at once Groups set # pages to be read, keep track on calendar	Teacher sets discussion schedule Two groups meet at once Groups meet once a week, set # pages to be read, calendar for reading, journals, discussion Groups keep track on bookmarks
Read & Prepare for Discussion *Chapter 5*	Read books w/ families or others over weekend or on Monday w/ school support Mark pages with Post-it Notes	Read during class 2–3 days a week Mark pages w/ Post-its Note interesting words, questions for discussion on bookmarks Collect Golden Lines (see Ch. 5) and respond in journals	Read during class 2–3 days a week Mark pages w/ Post-its Note questions/comments for discussion on bookmarks Respond in journal
Discussion *Chapter 5*	Teacher leads discussion Students share marked pages and comments	Teacher roams among groups; observes Teacher assigns "starter" who gathers books & journals and opens the discussion Students discuss marked pages, bookmarks, Golden Lines Whole class debriefs after discussion	Teacher sits near groups as observer Students manage own groups Students discuss marked pages, journal response, bookmark comments
Response Journals *Chapter 6*	Prompts/questions given early in year Students choose response later in year	Prompts/questions offered early in year Class brainstorms possible responses later in the year w/ guidance	Prompts/questions offered early in year Class brainstorms possible responses w/ guidance
Extension Projects *Chapter 8*	Teacher models one each week early in year Students choose project later in year	Teacher models & presents one project for each literature circle unit	Teacher models & presents limited choices early in year Students choose project later in year
Assessment *Chapters 5–8*	Anecdotal notes on discussion and response journals Rubric for extension projects	First time: No assessment Later: Anecdotal notes during discussion Rubric for discussion, response journals & extension projects	First time: Anecdotal notes during discussion Later: Rubric for discussion, response journals & extension projects

Figure 3.1 Literature Circle Structure in Three Classrooms

in and "built the airplane in flight." This may also happen to you. It seems reasonable that you may not know how a whole year will come together until *after* you've tried a few literature circle units[1].

Once you have some experience, you may be ready to align literature circles with your teaching and learning goals in a more deliberate way. Laying out a year's calendar will help you decide how many literature circle units will fit into your overall literacy program.

Figure 3.2 gives you an idea of how Janine King (6th grade) planned her year—once she had a handle on what she was doing. Notice how her teaching and learning focus (her goals) included literature circle processes, as well as literary elements and reading skills. Also notice the shaded area for May. Although she plans each year to culminate literature circles with an author study on Walter Dean Myers, Janine has never actually made it—a realistic example of planning challenges.

Month	Books Topic/Theme/Genre	Teaching/Learning Focus
September–October	Whole class: *Roll of Thunder, Hear My Cry*	Learning process of literature circles; Memorable language
November–January	Five books on homelessness Theme: Finding a Place to Belong (see Ch. 4 for book list)	Refining literature circles; Understanding theme; Fact vs. opinion; Stereotypes
February	Egypt	Refining literature circles; Reading non-fiction; Text elements: charts, graphs, glossary
March	Whole class: *Good Night, Mr. Tom*	Refining literature circles; Vocabulary; Using context clues
April May	Five books on the Japanese-American internment during WWII Theme: Swallowed by Injustice (see Ch. 4 for book list)	Refining literature circles; Understanding theme; Point of view; Author's craft
	Five books by Walter Dean Myers (see Ch. 4 for book list)	Refining literature circles; Author study; Voice

Figure 3.2 Literature Circles Calendar: Sixth Grade

[1]We define a literature circle unit as reading, responding to, and extending one book or set of books; also referred to as literature circle "rounds", "cycles", and "sets."

In the primary grades, especially when students are not yet reading independently, a unit can consist of one short picture book read, discussed, and extended in one week. In that case, several literature units might be presented before taking a break for other literacy instruction—then resuming literature circles in a month or so. Intermediate and middle grade teachers may offer three or four literature circle units a year. When just beginning, however, the same teachers might start with one round of literature circles, take several months off for other forms of instruction, and possibly resume with another round later in the year. As you plan your own timeline, keep in mind that you and your students will learn more with each literature circle unit. Therefore, the benefits will be greatest when not too much time passes between them.

What Should You Consider When Planning?

When and How to Begin   First, consider when in the year you want to begin. As an example, Vicki Yousoofian begins literature circles when she knows that her first graders have settled into the routine of Reading/Writing Workshop and are ready to add one more component. Usually, this occurs in late October or early November. Teachers of older students may find that they can begin sooner after taking several weeks of setting the groundwork to build collaboration, independence, and response as described in Chapter 2.

As they learn the processes of literature circles, students might read, discuss, write about, and respond to stories in a basal anthology or one whole-class book. Although Vicki has found that the stories in the anthology do not generate the same level of discussion as do trade books with more intricate plots, realistic characters, and memorable language, the anthology is a great place to begin, for the simple reason that she has one book for each child. Taking part in literature circles is demanding for students and teachers the first few times. While you and your students take the time to learn the processes, you may find that using books you have on hand works just fine.

Allow a Plan to Evolve   In reality, many teachers find that they can't lay out a whole year's plan *before* they begin literature circles. You may not have any idea how long each unit will take at first. You may even discover that one unit is all you can manage the first year. As we discussed in Chapter 1, literature circles will most likely evolve over time as you align your goals, the books you want to use, and the specific learning you want for your students.

Kirstin Gerhold experienced a common paralysis when she thought about the complexity of pulling everything together at once in her fifth grade classroom. She said, "There was no way that I could manage teaching my students how to do literature circles, *and* how to talk, *and* how to write in journals, *and* how to do an extension project all in one shot." So she started very simply. With each round of literature circles her first year, Kirstin added or refined only one or two components. Figure 3.3 shows how Kirstin's structure grew one step at a time. The shaded areas indicate where she focused her energies; the blank sections indicate what she ignored.

Putting the Pieces Together

Literature circle structure includes the following components: Choosing books and forming groups, reading, discussion, written and extended response, and management considerations.

	Book	Discussion	Journals	Extension Proj.
Round 1 **October**	*Call it Courage*: Chosen because it was available	Learning how to discuss		One project
Round 2 **November**	*Waterman's Boy*: Chosen because it came with the literature-based basal series	Developing discussion etiquette		Three options
Round 3 **January– February**	Five books about the Revolutionary War: Chosen because they fit a theme (see Ch. 4 for book list)	Refining discussions	Develop- ing under- standing of theme through writing	Whole class story quilt: Emphasis on extending the theme
Round 4 **May–June**	Four books about Growth and Change: Chosen because they fit a theme (see Ch. 4 for book list)	Developing understand- ing of theme through discussion		

Figure 3.3 Evolving Literature Circles Structure

Choosing Books and Forming Groups

Chapter 4 guides your selection of books for literature circle choices. But how do the students themselves decide which book they want to read, and how are the groups formed? Here are some considerations that will help:

Provide Choice   Most teachers discover that the best way to engender ownership and "buy in" for literature circles is to give students choice in the books they read. No matter what books you have chosen, scrounged, or discovered—allow students to select the one they want to read.

A key element of choice is offering a range of books that fit what you know about your students' abilities and interests. If your overall goal is for students to delve deeply into a book and construct meaning collaboratively with others, you'll probably want the groups to be heterogeneous by gender, experience, and ability. But there's a fine line between orchestrating diversity for its own sake and honoring students' choices. Most of the teachers we've worked with try very hard to keep student choice as their priority when forming the groups.

Introduce Books Through Book Talks   Informal introductions invite students to select and read a book by sharing just enough information to entice them without giving anything away. You might read aloud a short selection to give students a sense of the language and story. Better yet, ask students who have already read the book to give the book talk. This will be easier and more effective later in the year as more books have been read in your classroom.

Build in Time to Preview the Choices   Many teachers provide time for students to sample the book choices as they decide which one they want to read. If you give the book talks in the morning, for example, you might leave the books out during recess and lunch so that students can do a "hands on" perusal. Allowing enough time at this point is an effective way to honor your commitment to choice.

Teach Students How to Make Good Book Choices   We've all had students who chose a literature circle book for the reason that Hannah did: "Out of all those books, it was the only one calling my name." Students may need guidance to select books that call their names as well as books that they can read. Help students understand that making effective choices goes beyond finding the shortest (or longest) book. Selecting a book that holds your interest and gives you something worth discussing with others is part of becoming a critical reader.

There are several simple strategies for students to use as they choose a book that's right. Commonly known as the "five finger rule" or the "rule of thumb," one strategy is to pick up a book and begin to read anywhere. If you come to a word or place in the text that is hard, put up a finger. If you get to the end of a page or two and all five fingers are extended, the book may be too difficult for you. Another process (Ohlhausen & Jepsen, 1992) guides students to identify books that are "Too Easy," "Just Right," and "Too Hard."

During their book talks, many teachers set the books on the chalk tray or on a table, arranged according to difficulty. You do not need a readability formula to tell you how difficult a book will be for your students to read. Examine it. Flip through the pages. Look at the language, typeface—even the size of the print. Ask other teachers and students what they would say about its level. These informal—and quick—assessments can give you the information needed.

Guiding students to make good choices for themselves—and then honoring those choices yourself—is not always easy. If we decide what books are at a child's "reading level," then we're taking away choice. Sometimes, you may just have to trust a child to make a good choice—and then support her as she reads. Later in this chapter, you'll see how Lori Scobie helped her challenged readers as they read their literature circle books.

Students Select First, Second, and Third Choices   When students are ready to choose, distribute either pre-printed ballots or small pieces of blank paper on which students write their name and list one to three book choices. The key here is to help students understand that their first choice is the book they *most* want to read; their second and third choices should also be books that sound interesting and that they would be able to read if they cannot have their first choice.

Form Groups   Although student choice is at the core of literature circles, it is really *choice with teacher guidance*. You know your students well, and you should take the lead in forming the groups, taking into consideration what your students have chosen. Four to five members is an ideal group size—enough to generate discussion but not too many to stifle individuals. Janine King uses a simple and effective method for forming groups in her sixth grade classroom. The process takes about 10 minutes and can easily be done while students are at recess. She spreads out the ballots on a table to get an overview of which students have selected which books for their first choices. She writes the book titles on a tablet with five slots under each (Figure 3.4).

Janine keeps several things in mind as she makes decisions about assigning students to groups: Giving students their first choice as often as possible; making sure

Figure 3.4
Forming Groups
from Ballots

students in the group can work effectively together; providing some balance of gender, ability, experience, and interest; giving first choices to students who did not get them last time.

Determining How Much to Read

Another in a series of key decisions you will make comes right here: How many pages will your students read at a time? As you might expect, this will depend on many factors, such as your students' ages and abilities, their experience with literature circles, and the types of books they're reading (e.g., picture books or chapter books). Students need to read enough so that they have something substantive to talk about in their discussion but not too much that some students cannot finish. When they first begin, most teachers determine the number of pages each group will read. Gradually, many students can learn to set their own reading pace in collaboration with their group.

Here are some strategies to consider as you and your students make sense of the reading load:

Beginning Readers and Picture Books   Picture books for beginning readers are designed to be read in one sitting. Therefore, most primary grade teachers plan for a literature circle picture book to be read or reread in one day. For example, first grade teacher Vicki Yousoofian's students take their books home over a weekend to read with families, and then they reread their books on Monday prior to their discussions.

Easy Chapter Books   Short, illustrated chapter books, such as *Frog and Toad Together* (Lobel, 1979), make excellent transition books as students develop stamina for and interest in longer stories. Dividing these books by chapters often works well because it gives students larger "chunks" of text without overwhelming them.

Chapter Books   Once children move to chapter books of more than 100 pages, you can use a variety of ways to divide the reading. Many teachers ask students to read a chapter or two for each discussion. Others divide the book into thirds and schedule discussions about a week apart, providing several reading days for each segment of the book.

When your students are ready to set their own reading schedules, let them know the total amount of time they have available for reading and discussions—and let each group divide up their book.

Structuring Time for Reading

Time should be structured into the day for students to read their literature circle books. Students can do this independently, as partners, or in a larger group. Teachers often worry that inexperienced and challenged readers will not be able to participate fully in literature circles because the books are too hard for them. You may find that you need to make special accommodations so that all students *can* read their books and participate effectively in literature circle discussions. Here are some ways to help students who are either inexperienced or who have difficulties with reading:

Beginning Readers   Young students can accomplish the reading in a variety of ways. You can read the books with them during shared reading time. Then, they can read the books a second time with an adult volunteer, older reader, or at home with family members. Students can also read with a class partner. By this time, they have had several exposures to the book and it should be fairly familiar. First graders do not need to be able to read a book on their own in order to talk about it.

Challenged Readers   All of the teachers in this book are committed to literature circles because of the benefits they see for their students who are not strong readers. Mary Lou Laprade emphasizes the value of literature circles for one of her third graders: "When he read aloud, he would stumble and I know he was embarrassed. But when he sat at book club, he had some insights that none of the others had even thought of. He got the chance to hear books and discuss books that would have been out of his reach if he were stuck with the simple books at his own level." Guiding challenged readers through their literature circle books may include the strategies mentioned above as well as these: Provide additional time to complete the reading, read the book with resource teachers or other specialists, partner read the book with a classmate, listen to the book on tape and read along.

Structuring the Discussion

The format you select for discussions will depend on many things: your style, your students' ages and abilities, and needs that are specific to your classroom. You will certainly discover what best meets your needs as you and your students gain experience. Each of the formats described in Figure 3.5 has different benefits and challenges as the teacher assumes different roles.

One Group Meets at a Time with the Teacher as Facilitator   Most students need support as they learn to discuss books in literature circles. When this is the case, you may want to meet with each group to take on the role of facilitator, model, and guide. This format is comfortable—reassuring, even—for teachers at all grade levels as their students learn the process. Some teachers begin with this format and move on to one of the others; others keep this format all year.

This format allows for the greatest teacher control. However, it also may unintentionally encourage students to talk primarily to the teacher. Changing ingrained habits such as raising hands to speak may be more challenging when the teacher is always present in the group.

Like other first grade teachers, Vicki Yousoofian keeps this format all year (Figure 3.6). Students at this age are simultaneously learning to read and write *and* learning how to interact with others and books. For these reasons, teachers of early primary

Format	Teacher Role	Benefits	Challenges
One group meets at a time; other students work on reading, journal writing, extension projects	Facilitator	Control Opportunity to teach strategies for conversation and response May be an easier format for beginning literature circles	Students tend to talk to teacher, not each other Students not in discussion need to be able to work independently
One group meets at a time	Group member	Control Opportunity to model conversation and response Also a manageable format for beginning literature circles	Students tend to talk to teacher, not each other Students not in discussion need to be able to work independently
One group meets at a time	Removed observer	Control Opportunity to observe students' growth in discussion and response	Teacher's observation needs to be unobtrusive so that conversation is not stifled Students not in discussion need to be able to work independently
Two or more groups meet at a time	Observer and guide	Flexibility Opportunity to observe students' growth in discussion and response Greater input for discussion debriefings	Greater noise levels Teacher has less opportunity for in-depth assessment Possibility for chaos, unproductive behavior

Figure 3.5 Variations for Discussions

Figure 3.6 Teacher-Facilitated Group

grade students generally need to provide more overt teacher direction for literature circles than do some teachers of older students.

One Group Meets at a Time; Teacher Participates as a Group Member   This is a slight variation of the first format. As a group member, you have an excellent context in which to model conversation strategies and your own reading responses. When not assuming the role of facilitator, you may be more able to help students develop independent discussion strategies. Mary Lou Laprade moves to this format as her second and third graders learn to rely on each other in their discussions. She continues to sit with each group, but shifts to a role of participant rather than leader. As a model of conversation and response, Mary Lou still finds that some students need help as they learn not to direct their conversation to her alone.

One Group Meets at a Time; Teacher Sits Near and Observes   When Janine King first started literature circles, one group met at a time and she sat near them and took anecdotal notes on their discussions. As shown in Figure 3.7, Janine sat close enough to hear her sixth graders' conversation, but far enough away so that the students did not rely on her to run the group. She kept this format all year, even though her students became independent enough for several groups to meet at once. She felt strongly that this format allowed her to observe how the groups worked together, as well as gave her a wealth of insight into students' responses to the books. "I would miss out on so much rich discussion if I wasn't there," she said.

Figure 3.7
Student-Led Group
with Teacher as
Observer

Some teachers wonder if one student needs to take on the role of facilitator in order to keep things moving in the discussion. Although you may find that giving students specific roles in the discussion helps the groups get started, none of the teachers with whom we've worked use them or used them for long. Sometimes managing the roles takes so much energy and focus that students lose sight of their real purpose—to talk about books. However, if discussion roles would be helpful for you as you get started, we recommend the descriptions in Chapter 5 of Harvey Daniels' book, *Literature Circles: Voice and Choice in the Student-Centered Classroom* (1994).

Two or More Groups Meet at a Time; Teacher Roams as Observer and Guide   In Lori Scobie's fourth grade classroom, all groups meet at the same time for their discussions (Figure 3.8) because this is what seems most manageable to her. She can plan a set time each week when she knows that all groups will discuss.

Figure 3.8
Multiple Groups Meet at One
Time with Teacher as Observer

You may gradually move from one group meeting at a time to multiple groups as your students become adept and independent enough to manage discussions without your direct intervention. In fact, many teachers set this as their ultimate goal—multiple groups meeting at one time, a room filled with stimulating discussions. However, as we discuss in Chapter 5, learning to carry on a meaningful discussion is not easy for students at any age. In addition, the higher levels of activity—and noise—may not work for you. We urge you to start with the format that makes the most sense to you and fits what you know about your students.

Even when you plan a format that seems to work, don't be surprised if you change it as time goes on. Third grade teacher Adam Brauch started out with all groups meeting at once—not because it was the best format, but because it was the only one that occurred to him. However, he quickly discovered that he couldn't keep track of what was going on in each group. Adam realized he needed to meet with each group, first as leader, and then as a group member as his students learned the process of discussion.

Structuring Written and Extended Response

Other structural decisions you will make include organizing for written response and extending response through the arts. Later in this chapter, we walk through a first grade and a fourth grade classroom to show how two teachers structured journals and extension projects. Chapter 6 provides further detail about written response; Chapter 8 offers specific guidelines for extension projects.

Managing the Structure

Teachers describe the following as "little things that make a big difference" in managing literature circles:

Boxes to Hold Books and Journals   Many teachers find that chaos reigns when everyone scrambles to dig books and journals out of cramped desks before the discussion can begin. A solution: Foldable paper boxes such as those in Figure 3.9 keep each group's books and journals together. One student can be designated to gather the group's box as the other members move their chairs into their meeting position.

Figure 3.9 Book
and Journal
Boxes

Organizing Charts   Some teachers make and post a chart for each group listing the book title, members' names, and agreed-upon pages to be read each week (Figure 3.10). To identify the "starter" of each group's discussions, Lori Scobie attaches a clothespin next to one of the names on each group's chart. In her first year, she made charts for each group for each literature circle unit. In what she describes as a brilliant move, she laminated one large generic chart the next year. With a damp paper towel and an overhead pen, she can easily change the charts as the groups and books change.

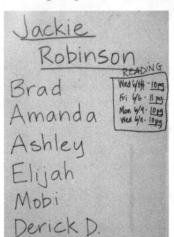

Figure 3.10 Group
Chart

A Glimpse into Two Classrooms

To clarify literature circles structure, let's take a look into two classrooms, grades 1 and 4. You'll meet two teachers who organize literature circles with some common components and some unique elements that suit their teaching styles, their students' ages and experiences, and the requirements of their schools. These examples should give you several ways to adapt structure to fit your own needs.

Vicki Yousoofian, First Grade

Vicki Yousoofian had been teaching first grade for five years when she began to use literature circles. Vicki's primary goal was to learn a new way to guide her first graders toward independence as readers and writers. In her classroom, literature circles play an integral role in the overall literacy program—they support her instruction in the technical aspects of reading. Through literature circles, students quickly catch on to one of the greater purposes of learning to read—to meet characters who can teach them about themselves and the world around them.

The structure presented here illustrates how Vicki organized literature circles during her first year. If you wandered into her classroom today, you would most likely see some of these structures in place—and others would be quite different. Vicki's structure—with greater teacher direction and a shorter time frame—is typical of how early primary teachers organize literature circles.

Planning a Timeline

One literature circle unit lasts from Friday to the following Friday (Figure 3.11).

Reading/Writing Workshop (10:00 a.m.–11:00 a.m.)

Friday	Monday—Tuesday—Wednesday	Thursday
Introduce books; Students choose by ballot Teacher forms groups Students take books home in plastic bag w/ Post-it Notes and parent letter Students present Extension Projects from previous week	Focus lesson on reading skill/ strategy Monday: Students may re-read literature circle book with peers, older students, adult volunteers Teacher meets with two literature circle groups per day for discussion and written response in Response Folders Other students select from "menu" of literacy activities (e.g., phonics practice, listening center, writing related to previous focus lesson)	Introduce and work on Extension Projects (to be presented the following day)

Figure 3.11 Literature Circle Weekly Calendar: First Grade

Choosing Books and Forming Groups

Vicki introduces the literature circle books on Friday morning. The selection process takes place throughout the day:

Introducing Books   Vicki introduces four to five books for literature circles. In her book talks, she discusses the theme of each book, indicates a general level of difficulty, and allows time for questions and comments. She reads a few pages (and at times the whole book) and encourages children to predict what the story will be about.

Forming Groups
Early in the year based on ability. During the first two rounds of literature circles, Vicki uses stories in the basal anthology to teach the literature circle process. At this time, all students read the same story. She forms her groups based on students' experience with reading, placing readers of similar ability in the same group.

Later in the year based on student choice. Later, when Vicki introduces several book choices, she forms groups based on student choice. On paper ballots, children write the titles of their first, second, and third choices. Vicki models the process for them, showing how she selects the book she would like to read the most (#1), and which ones she feels she could also read and would be interested in (#2 and #3). She explains to students that not everyone will get to read their first-choice book during literature circles. However, all of the books will be available during independent reading time throughout the week.

Vicki's method for forming groups is identical to the one Janine King uses (see Figure 3.4). During recess or lunch, Vicki sorts the ballots to form the groups. She matches students with books they have selected as their first choice as often as she can. With only four or five copies of each book, sometimes more students select a title than Vicki can accommodate in a group. In that case, she assigns students to a second or third choice. To honor her commitment to choice, Vicki keeps a record of students' book selections and knows which were first and lesser choices. This way, she will be sure to give students a first choice in the next round of literature circles.

Structuring Time for Reading

Vicki wants each student to have several exposures to the literature circle books throughout the week. In preparation for discussions, her students hear the books read aloud and read the books with family members over the weekend. Students also re-read the books independently, with Vicki or an adult volunteer, or with a classmate.

Read Aloud and Shared Reading   On Friday morning, Vicki reads several of the literature circle books aloud to the class. Students may also look at the books on their own and participate in shared reading activities with Vicki.

Reading with Families Over the Weekend   On Friday afternoon, children carry the books and one to three Post-it Notes home in large plastic bags. Vicki includes a letter to families that explains the objectives of literature circles and suggests ways family members can support the student's thinking and understanding. Vicki's letter is included at the end of this chapter.

Re-reading Literature Circle Books   On Monday morning, students also spend time re-reading the literature circle books, an important step for children who were not able to read at home. Vicki's adept readers re-read the books on their own or with a partner. For others, this is the time when she can tailor her guided reading instruction to those skills and strategies needed to read the literature circle book. Vicki may read the books with students or they may read with an older student or adult volunteer or listen to the book on tape.

Structuring the Reading/Writing Workshop

As shown in Figure 3.11, literature circles are part of the Reading/Writing Workshop in Vicki's classroom. This one-hour literacy block occurs every morning from 10:00 to 11:00. This instructional time includes a whole-class focus lesson on reading and/or writing strategies, a selection of literacy activities to reinforce skills and strategies, and literature circles.

Focus Lesson   First, Vicki conducts a short focus lesson on literacy strategies such as using phonics skills to identify unknown words, making predictions, using capitalization in writing, or responding personally to a story. These guided reading and writing lessons provide instruction in "how" to read and write.

Literacy Menu   Students who are not participating in the literature circle discussion work independently on the Reading/Writing Workshop Menu. The "menu" (Figure 3.12) consists of activities to provide practice with previously-taught phonics skills, handwriting, creative writing, and language strategies based on students' needs.

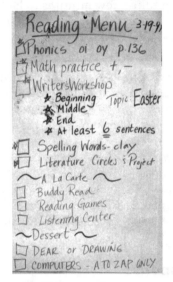

Figure 3.12
Reading/Writing Workshop Menu

Structuring the Discussion

Vicki meets with one or two literature circle groups each day. The actual discussion may last from 5 to 15 minutes. As students gradually learn more about what makes a discussion work, the time begins to stretch. Her simple gauge: Keep the discussion going only as long as someone has something to share.

As other students work on the literacy menu, Vicki calls a group to gather with her on a rug in one corner of the room. This helps children concentrate on the discussion but leaves Vicki free to observe what is going on with the rest of the students. Each discussion progresses the same way all year. This management technique helps Vicki build a discussion framework that is predictable for her students and helps them gradually internalize the elements of effective conversation. Here are the steps she uses:

Preparation   Each Monday morning, Vicki collects all of the books in their plastic bags and sets them on a shelf in the discussion corner. For each discussion, she has quick access to each group's set of books, a container of pencils, and each child's Reading Response Folder. The students bring nothing with them when they "come to the carpet." As a first step, Vicki asks for a "thumbs up" for a variety of questions: Are you sitting in a circle? Are your legs crossed? Did you read your story? Did you mark the pages you want to talk about?

Opening the Discussion   Throughout the year, Vicki begins each discussion with the same questions: "What is our purpose for literature circles? Why do we come together to talk about books?" Students' answers reveal how they grow in their understanding of literature circles. The responses evolve through the year from, "To talk about books" to "We learn what the character feels" and "We learn from each other."

As she hands out a book to each child, Vicki takes the time to focus students' attention on the basic literary elements of stories. She asks about the title and author of the book and for a brief summary of the main things that happened. Vicki may ask what happened at the beginning, middle, and end of the story. She may also ask one or two questions related to a theme or lesson in the book.

Reviewing Marked Pages   The children then take a few minutes to look at the pages they marked to help remind them of what they want to share in the discussion. When ready, students give her a thumbs up and close their books.

Modeling Skills of Conversation   Vicki's role in the discussion is that of a guide who models different ways to respond to books. For example, as a student shares the marked pages, Vicki shows the group how to focus attention on the speaker. At first, Vicki asks guiding questions to model what listeners might want to know about a book. She encourages everyone to add comments when the speaker finishes. In this way, she plants the seeds of what will later approximate real conversations.

Vicki looks for opportunities to point out when students begin to internalize strategies for discussion. For example, one day she noticed that Nick had gone beyond simply marking what he wanted to discuss. He came to his group with a few words written on one Post-it. Vicki pointed this out to the group and talked about how this helped Nick remember specifically what he wanted to say. She suggested that others might find this helpful.

Structuring Written and Extended Response

Reading Response Folders   At the end of the discussion, Vicki distributes the Reading Response Folders and puts the jar of pencils in the middle of the circle. The folders contain two forms of written response: A reading log to record the book title, author, and a short rating, and a Response Journal for more extended written response.

Reading log. The reading log provides a record of all of the books read in literature circles. On a simple form, students write the story title and rate how much they enjoyed the book.

Response journal. Vicki often gives a short prompt for writing (see Chapter 6), talking with children about possible journal entries they might write. To help students begin, Vicki reminds them to look through the pages of their books for ideas, perhaps finding something from the pages they marked and discussed. She finds that having the chance to discuss response ideas helps her young students get started. Students then return to their desks to write.

Vicki starts the year with limited choices for writing. At the beginning of the year, the written responses are often just a few sentences long. In many cases, students will draw a picture of something that was important from their book and then write a sentence or two about it. As students gain experience and confidence, she encourages them to use the journal prompt only if they have difficulty thinking of something to write.

As the year progresses, Vicki also adjusts the sequence of discussion and response journals. By January, for example, some students will come to the discussion first (groups that meet on Monday, for example) and then write in their journals; others will bring their journals to the discussion. Vicki find this works really well for first graders—some children need to talk about what they've read before they're ready to write; others need to write first.

Extension Projects Vicki introduces the week's extension project on Thursday. At the beginning of the year, when literature circle reading selections come from the anthology, these projects all relate to creative and artistic ways to build comprehension. For example, when students learned the structure of narrative (e.g., beginning, middle, end, problem, solution), the response project was a story hat (Figure 3.13) that illustrated narrative elements from the literature circle stories (see Chapter 8 for a detailed explanation of the story hat and other extension projects).

Figure 3.13
Story Hat
Extension Project

Later in the year, she introduces projects that are more focused on personal response: Story quilt (sample provided in Chapter 8), mural, readers theatre script, and accordion book. As with her written response choices, Vicki provides limited options in the fall. By winter and spring, Vicki introduces a new project each week, gradually offering a greater range of choices. Students may then select either that new choice or any of the previous projects.

Presenting Extension Projects In small groups, students share their extension projects on Friday. Each child tells the title and author of the story and describes the project and how it relates to the literature circle book. Children are encouraged to discuss why the book is an interesting one to read. When they have finished, the children evaluate their projects by writing what they were proud of and describing how they felt as they shared their project.

Now compare and contrast the structure that Lori Scobie uses with her older students. Whereas Vicki's literature circle units are completed in one week, Lori's stretch across several weeks. You will see, however, that there are many similarities in structure between these two classrooms.

Lori Scobie, Fourth Grade

Lori was a first-year teacher when she began literature circles. Looking back on that first year, she laughs and says, "I just assumed that *everybody* taught this way!" Her willingness to jump in and begin—even without much experience—is typical of her approach to teaching. Lori's goals, values, and knowledge of herself drove how she structured literature circles. She describes these as her "need for flexibility, desire to share responsibility with students, ability to deal with noise and chaos, and inability to stick to a tight schedule." Lori's structure is similar to what many later primary through middle grade teachers choose as a starting point.

Planning a Timeline

A Year's Calendar   Figure 3.14 shows the timeline for Lori's first year of literature circles with fourth graders. As we described in Chapter 1, this timeline evolved. Her first literature circle unit didn't begin until November and lasted over two months as she and her students felt their way through the process. Gradually, Lori became much better able to predict—and control—the timeline. Lori generally scheduled three to four weeks for each round of literature circles—three weeks for reading, responding and discussing; one week for extension projects.

Month	Book Selections & Topic/Theme/ Genre	Teaching/ Learning Focus	Books Chosen Because . . .
September– October		Developing a classroom climate in preparation for literature circles	
November– January	Whole class set: *Dear Mr. Henshaw*	Learning the structure of literature circles	Whole class set was available
February	Three choices: Humor books	Learning the structure of literature circles	Books were available and topic interested students
March–April	Four choices: Themed unit: Taking Action to Care for Others (see Ch. 4 for book list)	Refining structure Developing conceptual understanding: What it means to care for others	Books related to theme
May	Four choices: Biographies (see Ch. 4 for book list)	Refining structure Elements of biography	Books represented excellent examples of biographies
June		Wrapping up the school year	

Figure 3.14 Literature Circles Calendar: Fourth Grade

Weekly and Daily Schedules   With an overall timeline established (or at least a goal firmly in mind), Lori was able to manage the weekly and daily schedules by making the following decisions as in Figure 3.15.

Use the literacy block. Lori's literacy block is determined by her school—an hour and 15 minutes before the morning recess. It is a natural context for literature circles.

Plan a weekly schedule. Although the actual arrangement of components varied from week to week, Figure 3.15 shows a sample week's schedule during Lori's first year with literature circles.

Literacy Block—9:30–10:45 a.m.

Monday	Tuesday	Wednesday	Thursday	Friday

Read
Focus lesson
  on discus-
  sion pro-
  cedures
Discussion: All
  groups
Debrief
  discussion
	Focus lesson
	  on
	  reading
	  strategy
	Read
	Writing
	  linked to
	  strategy
	  lesson
		Journal
		  writing
		Focus lesson
		  on discus-
		  sion
		Discussion
		Debrief
		  discussion
			Focus lesson
			  on
			  reading
			  strategy
			Read
			Journal
			  writing
				Focus lesson
				  on
				  discussion
				Discussion
				Debrief
				  discussion
				Journal
				  writing

Figure 3.15 First Year: Sample Weekly Schedule

During the literacy block each week, students read their literature circle books two or three times and hold two or three group discussions. Students respond in journals on reading or discussion days. Lori teaches focus lessons each week on reading or writing strategies and discussion procedures. As students get farther into their books, Lori decreases the time spent reading and increases the time for discussions and debriefing.

In her first year, Lori's weekly schedule gradually changed as she and her students learned more about what worked for them. Early in the year, Lori placed a greater emphasis on focus lessons to teach literature circles procedures; later in the year, the focus lessons emphasized reading and writing strategies. Lori became better able to respond to the needs of her students as she made decisions about the timing and content of focus lessons.

In general, Lori says that each day includes "some mix of the following: Reading, writing about our reading, talking about our reading, talking about our writing, writing about our talking, and talking about our talking."

Choosing Books and Forming Groups

Lori's students select their literature circle books much as Vicki's first graders do. Lori presents each book to her students by giving a short book talk. Students fill out simple ballots and Lori makes up the groups. The process of choosing books takes place during a morning: about 20 minutes for the book talks; 20 minutes for students to sample the choices before, during, and after recess; 10 minutes for balloting after recess; and 20 minutes for Lori to form groups during lunch.

Structuring Formats for Reading

Like students in many fourth grade classrooms, Lori's represented a broad range of interests, abilities, and experiences: Strong and avid readers who devoured everything that came their way, reluctant readers with very limited interests, students severely challenged by reading because of disabilities or inexperience with English, and all those in between. Because of this, Lori used all of the following ways—singly and in combination—to encourage and support her students as they read literature circle books:

- *Independent reading*
- *Paired reading with a classmate*
- *Reading with an adult volunteer or older student*
- *Reading the book at home with family members*
- *Getting a head start on the literature circle book in the ESL or resource classroom*
- *Reading along with an audiotaped version of the book*

It is important to remember how literature circles fit into Lori's overall literacy program. Just as Vicki does, Lori spends considerable time both during and outside of literature circles developing students' technical expertise in reading and writing. One of her goals is for students to apply in literature circles what they are learning about reading. While working toward a thorough reading and understanding of the literature circle book, Lori knows that students' comprehension will also be developed through the discussion. In essence, literature circles provide multiple ways—including and in addition to reading—for students to construct meaning.

Structuring the Discussion

In the beginning, Lori decided that all groups would meet at the same time. It was the only way that made sense to her. Setting a schedule where only one or two groups met while other students read or worked on journals seemed far too complicated. To make this work, Lori's students needed to learn to hold their conversations without her as leader or facilitator—or even present. Contrast this with Vicki's discussions, which are completely teacher facilitated. The differences are not simply because Lori teaches fourth grade and Vicki first. Each teacher developed the discussion structure that fit her knowledge of herself, her students, and her teaching needs.

Lori understands that she cannot assume that students know everything they need to know in order to talk with one another. Here are some of the strategies Lori uses to structure the discussions in the beginning:

Establish Specific "Sites" for Discussion   To begin a discussion session, Lori directs her students to carry their chairs to designated places in the room. Once explained, modeled, and practiced, the process of "moving into groups" becomes more efficient as students learn where to go, how to get there, and how much time it should take.

Decide on the Teacher's Role   Notice how Lori's role in the discussions differs from Vicki's. Lori wants to maintain an oversight role when all groups meet at once. This allows her to roam among the groups, listening in on the conversations, and redirecting the discussion as necessary. From this vantage point, she gathers information to share with students during the whole-class debriefing that always follows discussion.

Appoint a "Starter" for Each Group   Although she didn't do this at first, Lori wishes she had. She soon discovered (as you may or have) that discussion groups can flounder if they have too little direction *or* if they have too much. After her first round of litera-ture circles, Lori assigned one person in each group to serve as the "starter." She does not want students to take on a more defined role as "group leader," whom other students might see as the person in charge. Lori wants everyone to take responsibility for the group's function. Therefore, the role of starter is fluid; Lori simply places a clothes-pin beside one person's name on a group chart (see Figure 3.10). The starter for that day brings the books and journals to the group and offers an opening comment or question. For Lori, designating a small role of starter is sufficient to get things going.

Debrief After Each Discussion   Lori makes sure that there is always time to bring the entire class back together following the discussion to talk about what went well and what skills need to be refined (see Chapter 5 for specific details on debriefing).

Structuring Written and Extended Response

Written response, either before or as a result of discussion, is an important component of literature circles in Lori's classroom. Lori's students use a Literature Response Log (see Chapter 5, Figure 5.9) for quick notes as they prepare for discussions. She also uses response journals following discussion.

Response Journals   To make the journals (Figure 3.16), Lori folds construction paper in half and staples several sheets of lined notebook paper to one side, a Golden Lines sheet to the other, and tucks a bookmark in the middle (see Chapters 5 and 6 for more information).

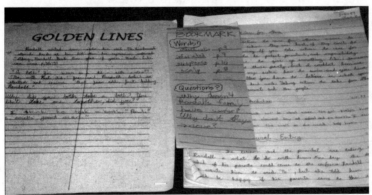

Figure 3.16
Response Journal

Writing in many forms and for a variety of purposes is pervasive in Lori's class-room. Her students are already familiar with journal responses by the time they begin literature circles. To elicit response specific to literature circles, Lori suggests prompts and questions similar to those described in Chapter 6. In addition, she and the students brainstorm other things to write about, and she invites students to select what works for them.

Extension Projects   Lori presents one extension project for each round of literature circles. Sometimes students do their projects individually, and sometimes everyone col-laborates on one large project. For example, when the whole class read *Dear Mr. Henshaw* (Cleary, 1983) the first year, each child contributed a page to an ABC Book describing key scenes in the novel represented by the letters of the alphabet. Later that year, each group worked on story quilt squares to illustrate how their different books fit a theme,

Taking Action to Care for Others. Finally, during the last literature circle on biographies, teams designed game boards on the challenges faced by famous people.

Some Final Thoughts on Structure

The bottom line on organizing literature circles is this: Your structure will most likely change with each new step you and your students take. Janine King said, "I think if you have a few basic plans and goals, and then take it from there, you can start. You're not going to accomplish everything the first year. I mean, in 20 years I'll still be re-doing them. And that's the reason I keep teaching."

What is worth worrying about?

- Be willing to jump in without knowing all of the answers—in fact, without even knowing all of the questions.

- Maintain realistic expectations for yourself and your students.

- Establish a framework for each component of literature circles in the first round; know that it will change over time.

- Invite your students to build the structure with you.

What is worth letting go?

- The belief that you have to know everything before you begin.

- The expectation that all components must work effectively the first few times.

Common Questions About Structure

What literacy activities can we do between literature circle units?
    Just like you, Lori Scobie is responsible for a wide range of reading and writing instruction. She knows that literature circles are not the appropriate venue for every aspect of literacy instruction. She also knows that her students cannot sustain the concentration and energy required to participate in literature circles for long stretches of time. They need to alternate literature circles with other forms of literacy work. After completing the literature circle unit on *Dear Mr. Henshaw* her first year, Lori spent several weeks using the literature anthology to work on reading strategies: Identifying unknown words, finding evidence in text to support a point, making and verifying predictions, and drawing inferences. Students used these strategies when they read and discussed their literature circles books; they also needed them for effective reading in social studies and science. Later in the year, Lori spent several weeks of her literacy block to develop students' research and writing skills for a class brochure about their native plant garden.

How important is it for me to share control with my students?
    Lori Scobie discovered that sharing control and decision making with her students made literature circles work more effectively more quickly. For example, she didn't know at the beginning how she could best manage the materials and keep track of groups—so she asked her students. Jim thought about this issue and came to class one morning with a solution: Have each student bring in a cereal box and cut them down for book and journal holders. He even figured out how big the boxes needed to be and how they could be cut to allow the most room with the greatest stability. Chapter 5 describes several ways that Lori and her students worked together to solve problems in the discussions. For every issue that arose, Lori's trust in her students allowed her to invite them into the solution.

I've got the overall structure—but can you give me an idea of how to plan the very first thing I should do?

As you're planning for that first week, keep in mind that you want to start slowly with one or two tasks for your students. Even just reading a selection, marking something to talk about, and moving into a group may be a big step. For the first discussion, maybe you just want to have students share something they marked and tell why they marked it. You might model this with the whole class before you have them try it in groups. We suggest you start as slowly (or jump in as quickly) as you feel ready. You can always—and *will* always—adjust as you go along.

How many discussions should I have a week?

As with most components of literature circles, this depends on many factors: Your total time frame for the literature circle unit, the difficulty of the books, and your students' level and experience. For the structure we've described in the primary grades, each group will most likely meet once a week. In the intermediate grades, groups may meet more often. Although you may begin by setting the schedule yourself, your students can help you figure out what works best. For example, Janine King's sixth graders learned how to set their own discussion schedules early in the process. Follow the suggestions in Chapter 3 for deciding how many pages to read a week, and that will help you decide how many discussions you will need to plan. One easy guideline: Let students discuss often enough to keep up their interest (talking with their classmates about the book will probably be their favorite part of literature circles), but allow enough time between discussions so that students will have read enough to have something to talk about.

How do I build in student ownership, responsibility, and independence?

This is a gradual process that begins long before you introduce literature circles (see Chapter 2 for specific strategies). As she developed her structure, though, Lori Scobie wanted each group to be responsible for setting how many pages they would need to read each day. She taught several focus lessons on how to divide the total number of pages in the book by the number of reading days. She also discovered that she needed to teach (and re-teach) focus lessons on compromise and making effective decisions that work for all group members. By expecting her students to take responsibility for their groups—and supporting them as they learned how to do this—Lori was able to guide students toward greater independence.

I've been collecting forms for students to use in their discussions, journals, and extension projects. But we seem to get bogged down in filling out the forms. What do other teachers do?

This was also a concern for Kirstin Gerhold: "I used a form that asked students to choose their favorite part of the chapter, ask a question, and find three words and write their definitions. My goal for having a form was so students could prepare for the discussion. But it turned out that the form became their main worry and headache because they spent all their time trying to find words and look them up." Kirstin fully realized how much the forms distracted students from her real purpose when one student told her, "I'm reading the book in bed at night, and my form's over there in my backpack, and I don't want to get out of bed to go get my form and find a pencil."

Another drawback to forms is that they can stifle conversations instead of inspire them. For example, Kirstin's students got in the habit of going around their discussion circle, each student reading the form. She says, "I was walking among the groups and listening as students asked their questions from the form. I just assumed that they would know to *answer* the questions. One group was going from person to person, 'My question is why did the main character . . .?' 'My question is . . .?' but no one answered the questions. I realized that they weren't using the form for a real purpose. So that's when I transferred to using just Post-it Notes."

See Chapters 5, 6, and 8 for suggestions on the judicious use of forms in discussions, written response, and extension projects.

How can I help families understand literature circles?

Vicki Yousoofian sends a letter explaining her goals for literature circles and how families can help their first graders read the books at home (see Vicki's letter at the end of this chapter). Other teachers provide information about literature circles in class newsletters, at Curriculum Night, or during parent conferences.

I want to be sure my students are busy and engaged—but I think I'm wearing them out with all the things I ask them to do. How can I cut back and still know that they're working hard?

Adam Brauch had this same experience with his third graders: "I had the kids do too much. They had to pick a passage they wanted to share, find five words, tell if they liked the book or not, do three prompts. It was a lot of work for them! It didn't really work and I didn't do anything with that information." When he thought about his major goal—to guide his students to talk about the books—Adam cut back on some of the tasks he assigned. Literature circles began to more closely meet his goals.

Letter to Families

Friday, November 7

Dear Families of Room 1B:

Literature circles are now a regular part of our reading program. On Fridays, I will introduce the book choices. Students will then select a book and bring it home to read over the weekend. The literature discussion groups will meet on Mondays and Tuesdays. Students will be expected to write about their books in their Reading Response Folders. In addition, some centers for the week will contain book extensions based on these books.

Your child has selected a book from several choices related by theme. Remember that because your child has self selected this book, it may not be a book at his or her independent reading level. Please read the book with your child, reading to them if necessary. The students will then share selections from their book in their group on Mondays. Eventually, the students will be leading the discussions of these books as well.

Here are some ways for you to read and discuss these books together in preparation for the group on Monday:

- Please have your child read (or read to him or her) and talk about the story as you read. Talking about the book will enhance your child's understanding.
- Read the book a second time and note favorite passages. Have your child use Post-it Notes to mark any pages that he or she would like to share and talk about in the group. What kinds of things should your child mark? Places that are funny, interesting, puzzling (things he or she doesn't understand), or passages that relate to his or her life. Your child may want to mark a place where he or she notices author's style, something about one of the characters, the main idea of the story, or certain details or illustrations.
- If possible, your child should be prepared to read the selected part(s) to the group. Our goal is that by the end of the year, all students will be participating in this manner.
- Send the book back to school on Monday with the pages marked.

Thank you for your support and assistance! I look forward to the many discussions this year that will expand and promote our love of reading.

Sincerely,
Vicki Yousoofian

CHAPTER 4

Good Books for Literature Circles

I wish I read a book and it was such a good book I wanted to go inside. So I can just stick myself inside and do what they are doing. If they are doing a big party then I would eat the whole thing.

—Michael's journal entry, fifth grade

Michael knows what we need for literature circles—books that grab readers and make them want to "eat the whole thing." Find books that capture your students, and you solve many of the challenges you will face with literature circles. How do you do that? This chapter gives you some things to think about when looking for books for literature circles and suggests places to start, keeping in mind the reality that you may not have access to a lot of "eatable" books right at first.

The chapter tackles the following questions:

- What makes a good literature circle book?
- What books do I start with?
- How do I find books to fit a range of reading abilities and interests?
- How do I get multiple copies?
- What are some good book sets to use?

What Makes a Good Literature Circle Book?

A good literature circle book touches something within the reader's heart and mind and compels response. You can use some fairly simple criteria to help you find such books. For example, consider these three questions: "Does the book succeed in arousing my emotions and will it arouse children's emotions? Is the book well written? Is the book meaningful?" (Monson, 1995, p. 113). In short, a good literature circle book has substance—something worth talking about.

In addition to content, consider a book's layout—number of pages, size of print, inviting space on the page, use and placement of illustrations. These can be crucial deciding factors for students as they choose a book. If the configuration of pages and print is too overwhelming, a book may seem insurmountably difficult even though its content is riveting. As veteran teacher Dan Kryszak told us, "You can tell a well laid-out book, as if it says, 'Hey, I've got a great story. Come on in and relax and enjoy it' not 'Here it is—BAM. Hurry up or you'll never finish!'"

How can you tell if a book will work? Here are some specific considerations that teachers make when choosing books for literature circles:

- **Compelling content—action, suspense, dialogue, humor, controversy:** Most teachers look for books in which the story blasts off from the first few pages. Books with action and conflict automatically prompt response. As Janine King said, "If students disagree with what the characters are doing, they'll talk. If they think the character's making some bad choices, they can get pretty riled up and want to talk about that, too."

- **Realistic characters:** As readers, we all want characters we can come to know, characters so real that they could walk down the street with us.

- **Picture books with strong, colorful illustrations that support the story:** Illustrations can be as important as story content in sparking response, particularly for beginning readers.

In short, good books for literature circles answer Charlotte Huck's enduring question, "Why literature?":

Because literature has the power . . .

- To make us more human, to help us see the world from inside the skin of persons very different from ourselves; to live more lives than the one we have; to try on various roles.

- To develop compassion and insight into the behavior of ourselves and others (through characters so real that the reader lives and suffers and rejoices with them).

- To show us the past in a way that helps us understand the present.

- To move us in ways that facts, statistics, and history texts can rarely do.

- To develop the imagination; to help us entertain ideas we never could have had; to interpret and translate our experiences, to shape our world, and to enlarge our imaginations.

- To take us out of ourselves and return us to ourselves as a changed self; to enlarge our thinking while educating our hearts.

(1987, pp. 69–71)

Figure 4.1 "Why Literature?"

What Books Do I Start With?

We approach this from two perspectives: How to choose books *the first time* you do literature circles, and how to select books later. It's important to accept that the first few times you may not be able to find "perfect" literature circle books. Nearly every teacher with whom we've worked started out with books that were on hand then gradually found books that met the criteria for quality described above.

Here are some possible ways to choose your first literature circle books:

Think about your goals: Chapter 1 described Vicki Yousoofian's goal for her first round of literature circles—"just to start." To begin, Vicki chose the material she had closest at hand: the basal anthology. She found a story that would reinforce reading skills she was already teaching. On the other hand, Adam Brauch knew his school library had a class set of *Bunnicula* (1979) by Deborah and James Howe, so he chose that. He wanted something funny that he knew his third graders would enjoy. His goal was to entice his students into literature circles through humor. Because Janine King's goal was for students to begin their discussions with a substantive book right off the bat, she took time to find just the right book before she started literature circles. Janine selected Mildred Taylor's *Roll of Thunder, Hear My Cry* (1976) because she knew it had the depth and drama she sought.

Begin with what you have in your classroom: Sometimes it's not your goals that drive your choice of books. You may start with a story in the basal anthology or it may be one book that everyone reads because that is what's available or simply because there are enough copies for everyone. In order to begin, you may have to settle for a less-than-perfect book. But at least you can begin.

Find out what is available in your school: Your teaching colleagues and the school librarian can be excellent sources of good books that have worked in other classrooms. One of the most effective book-finding strategies is what we call "Walk the School." Gather your colleagues and literally walk through your school, looking in bookshelves, opening closets, scanning the entire building for books that surely are there but have been long overlooked. You may be surprised at the literature treasury you unearth.

Check out other resources: Journals, professional books, and web sites abound with detailed and helpful book reviews and suggestions for literature circles:

- *Professional Books*   Many professional books include book lists. You might start by looking through a text you or a colleague used in a children's literature course. In addition, the annotated bibliography in *Literature Circles and Response* (Hill, Johnson, & Schlick Noe, 1995) offers high-quality books organized by themes. The list includes picture books, easy chapter books, novels, informational books, and poetry. You will also find helpful suggestions in professional books that are not necessarily written about literature circles. For example, Regie Routman's *Invitations: Changing as Teachers and Learners K-12* (1991, 1994) provides an extensive list of children's and young adult literature categorized by grade level (pp. 103b–166b). A effective resource for multicultural literature is Violet J. Harris's edited book, *Using Multiethnic Literature in the K-8 Classroom* (1997). In addition, an excellent resource for picture books is Ruth Culham's *Picture Books: An Annotated Bibliography with Activities for Teaching Writing* (1998).

- *Journals*   The professional journals we rely on for book suggestions include *Book Links* (American Library Association); *The Horn Book Magazine*; monthly columns in *The Reading Teacher* and *Journal of Adolescent and Adult Literacy* (International Reading Association), *Language Arts* and *Journal of Children's Literature* (National Council of Teachers of English), and *The New Advocate*.

- *Web Sites and Computer Resources*   A growing number of Internet sites provide excellent resources for literature. For example, *Book Links* magazine is now available online through the web site of the American Library Association (http://www.ala.org). Perhaps the most comprehensive web site is The Children's Literature Web Guide (http://www.acs.ucalgary.ca/~dkbrown/index.html). This site can best be described as the gateway to most other web-based resources you would need for literature circles. All of the major children's and adolescent literature award winners are included, such as the Newbery and Caldecott Medals; the Coretta Scott King Award; Notable Trade Books in the Field of Social Studies (National Council for the Social Studies); and Children's, Teachers', and Young Adult Choices (International Reading Association).

A useful computer resource for book selection is *The Horn Book Guide, Interactive* (1998), a CD-ROM listing over 29,000 short reviews of children's and young adult literature from *The Horn Book Magazine*.

How Do I Find Books to Fit a Range of Reading Abilities and Interests?

An intermediate teacher told us recently, "I would love to do literature circles on a theme . . . but I have kids reading at every level. I would need to find two or three books at the first grade level, half a dozen at the second or third grade level, about fifteen at fourth grade, and a handful that were even higher. Can I do this?" Does this sound familiar? You have to let go of the idea that you must find books written specifically for a given grade level. Remember that one of the benefits of literature circles is that they allow students to work together to understand and enjoy books. Therefore, students can respond to books in literature circles that aren't necessarily right at their independent reading level.

We suggest that you pursue books with a range of difficulty the same way you look for any book—talk with colleagues and your students, look at the books themselves, help your students learn to choose books that work for them. Comb all of the book resources we suggest in this chapter. And try out the book sets that we recommend. At each grade level, we have included books that are easier to read and also more challenging.

How Do I Obtain Multiple Copies?

Teachers use some or all of the following ways to obtain multiple copies of books for literature circles:

- Share book sets with other teachers at your grade level in your school and perhaps neighboring schools;
- Use bonus points from your students' book orders to buy book sets;
- Work with your school and public libraries to gather multiple copies;
- Obtain grants through your Parent/Teacher/Student Association to buy books;
- Search bazaars, garage sales, and bookstores that sell used books.

What Are Some Good Book Sets to Use?

We asked this question of the teachers who collaborated on this book. The lists that follow represent good "getting started" sets of books at a range of grade levels. We offer them as catalysts for early literature circles, knowing that you will certainly have others to add as you and your students discover which books work best. Figure 4.2 shows book sets organized by theme, topic, or author. Any of the books listed here would also be great "jumping off" books to use as a whole-class set.

1st Grade	4th Grade
Friendship	***Taking Action to Care for Others***
Officer Buckle and Gloria by Peggy Rathmann	**Picture Books**
Chrysanthemum by Kevin Henkes	*Sweet Clara and the Freedom Quilt* by Deborah
Ruby the Copycat by Peggy Rathmann	Hopkinson
Babushka's Doll by Patricia Polacco	*Prince William* by Ted and Gloria Rand
Relationships with Elders	*Uncle Jed's Barbershop* by Margaree King Mitchell
Now One Foot, Now the Other by Tomie De Paola	**Novels**
Wilfrid Gordon McDonald Partridge by Mem Fox	*Thunder at Gettysburg* by Patricia Gauch
The Quilt Story by Tony Johnston	*Journey to Jo'burg* by Beverly Naidoo
A Chair for My Mother by Vera B. Williams	*Randall's Wall* by Carol Fenner
Thunder Cake by Patricia Polacco	*Snow Treasure* by Marie McSwigan
Retold Fairy Tales	***Biographies***
The Frog Prince Continued by Jon Scieszka	*Lost Star: The Story of Amelia Earhart* by Patricia Lauber
Emperor Penguin's New Clothes by Janet Perlman	*Sojourner Truth: Ain't I a Woman?* by Patricia and
Cinder Edna by Ellen Jackson	Fredrick McKissack
Cinderella Penguin by Janet Perlman	*The Story of Jackie Robinson: The Bravest Man in*
The True Story of the Three Pigs by Jon Scieszka	*Baseball* by Margaret Davidson
Jim and the Beanstalk by Raymond Briggs	*Helen Keller: Courage in the Dark* by Johanna Hurwitz
2nd Grade	**5th Grade**
Caring for Animals and the Environment	***Revolutionary War: Facing Hard Times with Courage***
Picture Books	*My Brother Sam is Dead* by James Lincoln Collier and
Prince William by Ted and Gloria Rand	Christopher Collier
Where Once There was a Wood by Denise Fleming	*George Washington's Socks* by Elvira Woodruff
The Great Kapok Tree by Lynne Cherry	*Johnny Tremain* by Esther Forbes
A River Ran Wild by Lynne Cherry	*The Fighting Ground* by Avi
Non-Fiction	*Sarah Bishop* by Scott O'Dell
Be a Friend to Trees by Patricia Lauber	***Growth and Change***
There's an Owl in the Shower by Jean Craighead	*The Great Gilly Hopkins* by Katherine Paterson
George	*Maniac Magee* by Jerry Spinelli
One Day in the Woods by Jean Craighead George	*The Pickle Song* by Barthe DeClements
Chapter Books	*There's a Boy in the Girls' Bathroom* by Louis Sachar
Shiloh by Phyllis Reynolds Naylor	
Stone Fox by John Reynolds Gardiner	
3rd Grade	**6th Grade**
Challenges	***Homeless Children***
Aldo Applesauce by Johanna Hurwitz	**Picture Book**
Family Under the Bridge by Natalie Savage Carlson	*Fly Away Home* by Eve Bunting
The Chalk Box Kid by Clyde Robert Bulla	**Novels**
The Boxcar Children by Gertrude Chandler Warner	*Randall's Wall* by Carol Fenner
Freckle Juice by Judy Blume	*Homecoming* by Cynthia Voigt
Humor	*Monkey Island* by Paula Fox
Amelia Bedelia by Peggy Parish	*Maniac Magee* by Jerry Spinelli
Henry and Mudge by Cynthia Rylant	*A Place to Call Home* by Jackie French Koller
The Chocolate Touch by Patrick Skene Catling	*When the Road Ends* by Jean Thesman
Nate the Great by Marjorie Sharmat	**Informational Book**
Bunnicula by Deborah and James Howe	*Home: A Collaboration of Thirty Distinguished Authors*
Author Study: James Marshall	*and Illustrators of Children's Books to Aid the Homeless,*
Yummers!	edited by Michael J. Rosen
Yummers Too!	***The Japanese Internment***
Three Up a Tree	**Picture Book**
Author Study: E. B. White	*The Bracelet* by Yoshiko Uchida
Stuart Little	**Novels**
Charlotte's Web	*The Eternal Spring of Mr. Ito* by Sheila Garrigue
Trumpet of the Swan	*Farewell to Manzanar* by Jeanne Wakatsuki Houston
	The Invisible Thread by Yoshiko Uchida
	The Moved-Outers by Florence Crannell Means
	Journey to Topaz by Yoshiko Uchida
	Author Study: Walter Dean Myers
	Scorpions
	Somewhere in the Darkness
	The Glory Field
	Slam!
	Malcolm X: By Any Means Necessary

Figure 4.2 Book Sets by Grade Level

Although these books are identified by the grade levels in which they were used, we know that a specific book will work well for a range of students. This was made clear to us when Lori Scobie (fourth grade) and Janine King (sixth grade) both chose Carol Fenner's *Randall's Wall* (1991) for literature circles. The book was a tremendous success in both classrooms, even though Lori's students were younger and much less adept readers than Janine's. *Randall's Wall* is a good example of a fairly short, easy-to-read book that is accessible to less experienced readers and also has the depth and well-developed characters to satisfy stronger readers.

Some Final Thoughts on Good Books

Everything can fall into place more smoothly when you combine good books and literature circles. Books with "meat on their bones" can entice young readers almost as irresistibly as a siren's song. Begin with what you can find . . . and build from there.

What is worth worrying about?

- Balance your search for the *right* books with finding *something* with which to begin.

- Use all resources at hand—your own shelves, your colleagues, your school and public libraries, book order bonus points, used-book stores and garage sales—to obtain books for literature circles.

What is worth letting go?

- The feeling that you must have the perfect book before you begin.

A Question About Books

I found five books I want to use, but I haven't read them all. Will that be a big problem?
You'll always feel more in control of literature circles when you use books you've selected because you think your students can read them, will enjoy them, and will learn something from them. It helps to have read them yourself before you begin. Realistically, that's not always possible. Adam Brauch found that to be both frustrating and useful: "It was uncomfortable when I hadn't read all of the books—I felt like I was faking it. I could have provided better direction, even subtly, if I'd known the material. However, not knowing the books helped me ask real questions when I met with the groups." We suggest that you make every effort to read the books—then find knowledgeable colleagues and students to fill you in on those books that you cannot get to.

CHAPTER 5

Discussion

*We believe that genuine meaning, meaning over which readers have own-
ership, arises only if readers are able to structure it themselves, through
their own interpretations, in light of their experiences and their intent. It
is in this way that the text is brought to life.*

—Ralph Peterson and Maryann Eeds,
Grand Conversations (1990, p. 18)

Talking is one of our most personal and natural responses to reading. When you
finish a good book, don't you long to talk with someone about it? Sharing with others is
a treasured part of reading; for many of us, the experience is not complete without it.
And through talk, we "bring the text to life."

Discussion is at the heart of literature circles. Effective discussions increase students' understanding of what they read, as well as make the reading experience more
enjoyable. Those of you who have been in (or have longed to join) an adult book group
know this. When you have the opportunity to explore a book with other readers, that
collaboration may help you discover aspects of the book that you might have missed on
your own. Sixth grade teacher Janine King found a direct relationship between her own
experiences in a book group and what she hopes will occur for her students in literature
circles. "When we had our book group, I thought I was getting a lot out of the book," she
said. "But the group helped me look at it in new ways. What I may have glossed over,
someone else found riveting. That's what the discussion did for us."

Now, think about how talk changes when you are in a classroom. The language we
use to interact with one another in school often loses the spontaneity—that *magic*—of
conversations around the dinner table, on the sidewalk outside the theater, in the com-
pany of good friends. How can we make talking about books in school as exciting, natural, and effective for learning as it can be in those settings?

This chapter presents several ways to organize discussions to help students construct meaning collaboratively, strengthen individual understanding, and increase engagement with literature circle books. We will explain how to guide students to gather
ideas for discussion from their reading. We will also describe ways to teach students the
conversational arts that take discussion from rote recitation to real interaction among
readers.

First-year teachers Adam Brauch and Kirstin Gerhold knew they needed an organized approach to discussion in order for literature circles to succeed. Working together,
they developed a blueprint shown in Figure 5.1 for making discussions work in their
third and fifth grade classrooms.

In order to begin, you need a clear idea of what you are trying to accomplish through
discussion.

Making Discussions Work

Clarify goals for discussion—for yourself and for your students

Select a discussion format
- One group meets at a time with you as the leader
- One group at a time; you participate as a group member
- One group at a time; you sit near and observe
- Two or more groups meet at a time; you roam among them as an observer

Help students find what to discuss
- Brainstorm possibilities
- "Question and quote"
- Prompts
- Student-generated questions

Show students how to gather information to share in discussion
- Post-it Notes
- Bookmarks
- "Golden Lines"
- Discussion logs

Teach students *how* to discuss
- Brainstorm: Identify what works and what doesn't in discussion
- Develop guidelines and ground rules for discussion
- Teach elements of effective discussion
- Model
- Practice
- Reflect and debrief to refine guidelines and build strategies

---

Figure 5.1 Making Discussions Work

What Are Your Goals for Discussion?

Think about what you want students to gain from discussing books with one another. Your overall goal will influence how you teach the art of discussion. For example, consider two goals that have opposite implications for literature circles: (1) My main goal is to teach comprehension skills and strategies; therefore, I'll look for evidence of understanding and answers to questions in the discussion. (2) My main goal is for my students to engage in genuine conversations about books; therefore, I'll help them learn how to do that and will support them in constructing personal meaning and response.

When getting started with literature circles, many teachers focus more on developing children's reading skills and strategies than on their motivation to read and personal construction of meaning. Therefore, literature circle discussions may start out looking more like traditional reading groups than actual conversations. What we have found, however, is that literature circles can quickly become routine and boring with this limited focus.

If you see discussions as only a means to teach or assess comprehension, you may be disappointed in the results. The teachers we work with teach comprehension skills and strategies in need-based focus lessons (see Chapter 7) or in settings outside of literature circles.

Your most effective goals for discussion can come from your students themselves. Fifth grade teacher Patricia Kamber (1995) introduced discussion by asking her students, "Why do we talk about books?" Her students' comments grew into a chart (Figure 5.2) that hung prominently in their classroom.

Reasons to Talk About Books

To voice our ideas
To learn about other people's ideas
To sort out our ideas and toss them around and see how they turn out
To understand ourselves and each other together
To understand the world better

Figure 5.2 Reasons to Talk About Books

Invite students to help you create a classroom chart of reasons to talk about books. You may need to begin the conversation by sharing why *you* enjoy talking about books with others. As students recognize that talk plays a key role in their growth as readers and in their love of reading, they will begin to understand the benefits—and goals—of discussion in literature circles.

Selecting a Discussion Format

Chapter 3 described several discussion formats that might work in your classroom (see Figure 3.5):

- One group meets at a time with the teacher as the facilitator

- One group at a time; teacher participates as a group member

- One group at a time; teacher sits near and observes

- Two or more groups meet at a time; teacher roams among them as observer/facilitator

As we discussed in Chapter 3, many teachers find that having one group meet at a time is a simple and manageable structure early in the process. Some move on to a format where several (or all) groups meet simultaneously as everyone gains confidence and experience. However, other teachers stay with the one-group structure all year because it gives them more in-depth opportunities to observe and provide guidance and feedback.

Once you have settled on a format with which to begin, talk with students about how this format will help them meet your goals for discussion. You may also want to involve your students in determining a format that makes sense to them. This offers an excellent opportunity for students to practice the decision-making skills that they'll use throughout the literature circles process. Whether you make the decision or make it jointly with your class, is up to you. Some teachers feel comfortable sharing this decision—and others just want to settle on one format and begin.

A Discussion Framework

Students need something to talk about during literature circles—or you will have silence or chaos. Carrying on a real conversation is a complex undertaking. If talking in this context is new, students will need guidance on what and how to discuss.

Therefore, you may need to teach discussion skills that fit your students' experience and ability. You may also need to help students develop guidelines for discussions and learn how to gather ideas from books. Students at all levels will need to know:

What do I talk about? What have I read that intrigues, saddens, worries, puzzles me and will be interesting to my group?

How do I gather information to share? How can I keep track of quotes I like, interesting words, or events that happen in the book that I want to talk about?

How do I participate in a discussion? How can I be both a good listener and an active contributor?

What to Talk About

The most important aspect of finding something to talk about is this: What is meaningful to *you*? This will certainly vary for each reader. Discussions will not be very authentic if students only answer questions that teachers give them. Students need to read for themselves, to bring their own ideas, puzzlements, discoveries, and insights to the literature circle. This is the only way they will reach your overall goal of having genuine conversations about literature.

Adam Brauch's third graders brainstormed the following list of things to discuss:

Share a part of the book: favorite, confusing, interesting, surprising, scary, difficult
Make a connection
Read or tell about a journal entry
Pose a question
Answer a question

As with other lists in this book, you may be tempted to copy this list and present it to your students. But don't. These strategies fit Adam's class. Your students can generate a list that is meaningful to them—inspiring greater ownership and motivation to use it.

Getting Started: An Open Invitation   The simplest form of response to literature is a personal reaction: "What did you think of the story?" An open-ended question such as this one is a great way to begin. Vicki Yousoofian knew that her first graders were eager to offer their reactions. She also knew that this was a familiar form of response and would be an easy way to introduce them to discussion. This question generated a flurry of comments during her first literature circle: "It made me happy because the owl tried to wake everyone up." "It made me feel like I was at home." "I liked the bees buzzing."

Next Steps   First graders (and many others) will easily tell you what they liked about a story or book. However, a real conversation needs more than reactions—it needs interaction. You might try these "next step" strategies as you guide students to find something to talk about:

Quote and question. As students read, ask them to find one quote that stood out for them and one question that genuinely puzzled them.

You can model this with a picture book or with your read-aloud chapter book. Talk through your own thinking and show how you notice phrases, events, dialogue that captured your interest. Then, generate some questions together. At first, students may ask "teacher questions" such as, "Who was the main character?" But when you share questions that occurred to you as you read, you model the kinds of "real" questions that push us into conversations: "Why would he have . . .?", "I don't understand how . . .", "I would have done it differently—what do you think?"

Prompts. Simple prompts can also help students find discussion-worthy nuggets. Students can write these prompts in their journals and think about them as they read. For best results, begin slowly: Offer two or three prompts, talk with students about the kinds of information each would elicit, and model your own use of the prompts before sending students off to use them on their own. As students feel more comfortable with these prompts, add a few more. *Better yet*, ask your students to think up some prompts that they would like to use.

Adam Brauch did this with his third graders. After a week of using a few of the open-ended prompts, Adam asked his students what they might add to this list. They came up with their own ideas, which they then used and expanded throughout the year. Adam quickly realized that the students' prompts were much more interesting and meaningful to them than the ones he had suggested. Figure 5.3 shows the chart of prompts created by Adam's class.

Figure 5.3 Third Graders'
Expanded Prompts

As with all aspects of the discussion, however, you must remember that spontaneous conversations are the goal. Every support tool that we offer can be very helpful as students approximate this goal—but they can also be overdone. You may experience this when you hear in a discussion, "My favorite part was when the troops discovered the boy. My question is, 'Why didn't he run away?' What if . . ." Stringing together prompts rather than elaborating on one in depth tells you that students haven't fully internalized the purpose of the prompts. The value of any of these tools is to provide initial scaffolding while students become comfortable with discussion—but prompts can quickly detract from the conversation when they become the focus themselves.

Guided topic. You may also want to suggest a topic for discussion that you introduce through a focus lesson. When Lori Scobie's students explored the theme, Taking Action to Care for Others, she asked students to talk about evidence of how the characters in their books cared for one another. This is an effective way to guide students as they learn to find their own discussion topics. It may also help them pull out information that you know is important in their books. However, this strategy should be used sparingly so that literature circles do not become just teacher directed. You might suggest that the discussion *also* include your topic to let students know that yours is only one possibility for their conversation.

Student-generated questions. Generate a list of open-ended questions with your students. Such questions have many possible answers and allow for readers' differing interpretations and opinions. Like prompts, a list of questions is only a beginning point—encourage students to use them only when they do not easily find their own things to talk about.

Lori Scobie's fourth graders came up with the questions in Figure 5.4 for both journals and discussion. To generate this list, Lori asked her students, "What are some things you would really want to know when you talk with someone about your book?" Students took turns suggesting and writing the questions on a large sheet of chart paper. Then, as students read their literature circle books and as the groups met for the first few times, the chart was available for ready reference. However, Lori discovered that the children quickly internalized these questions. Within a week or so, the chart was no longer needed.

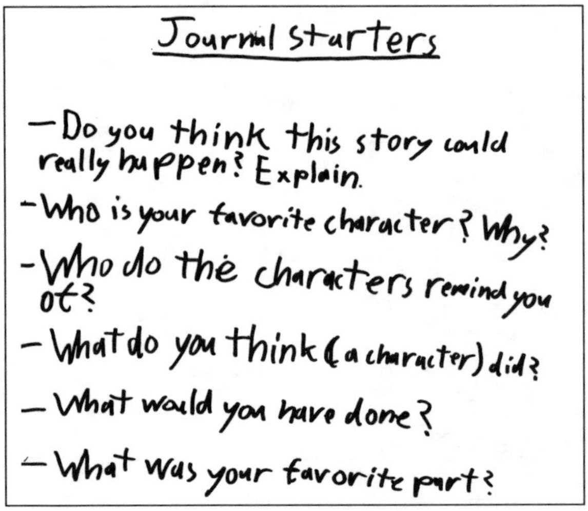

Figure 5.4
Student-Generated Questions

Younger students can also generate their own open-ended questions. Vicki Yousoofian tried this with her first graders early in the year. Some of the questions they wanted to ask:

What did you like about the story?
Where did the story take place?
Was the story real?
What happened at the beginning (middle and end)?
Do you think other kids would like this story? Why?

You might want to begin with some of the examples we have given here. But you will certainly want to involve your own students in generating the bulk of the discussion possibilities for your classroom. In addition, help your students recognize when they're ready to leave a list of questions behind completely after they have been fully internalized. For example, as Janine King listened in on a discussion of Mildred Taylor's *Let the Circle Be Unbroken* (1981), she heard questions such as these: "Why is the book called *Let the Circle Be Unbroken*?" "Why doesn't Cassie like Suzella?" Janine knew it was time to put away the list.

Another caution involves quantity: Students who are new to discussions can become overwhelmed by too many questions or prompts. Vicki Yousoofian made this discovery when she posted a list of 25 questions. The children had a hard time wading through the list to find questions to ask one another. Vicki realized that she needed to offer fewer questions at a time and to teach her students how to ask the ones that really mattered to them.

Begin slowly and find a balance between too few and too many structures for discussion. You may discover that your students can soon take off on their own and no longer need the temporary scaffolding of the questions and prompts. That is when you know literature circles are beginning to work.

Gathering Information to Share

The purpose for gathering information to share in the discussion is simple: Before you talk, you do some thinking about what you've read and what you want to talk about with others. As they read, students search for events that move them, funny parts that make them chuckle, places where the characters reveal themselves, interesting language and style that authors use. "Reading with an eye toward discussion" means that you read to find something worth sharing with others. When getting started with literature circles, many students need some help; as they gain experience, readers will find their own strategies.

Gathering information and keeping track of it involves several simple, yet effective, tools:

Post-it Notes The best—though unintentional—invention for literature circles is the Post-it Note. These small "flags" work well to identify passages that students want to share in a discussion. They are portable, adhesive, and removable—creating a tool for gathering information during reading that can be used more than once. As they read, students can make short notes or write questions on the Post-it to remind them of what they want to discuss. Figure 5.5 shows an example.

Figure 5.5
Post-it Notes in
Sixth Grade

Part of preparing for a discussion is knowing what you want to say. The Post-it Notes act as a bridge between the time students discover something they want to talk about and the time they can get to the discussion. Janine King guides her sixth graders:

"You have these things as you're reading that you know you're going to want to talk about. But you can't remember them a few days later. Marking passages reminds you of why this paragraph or conversation struck you—why it made you stop and think, 'Yeah, I want to talk about this.'" Janine then shows her students how she writes on her own Post-it Notes as she prepares for her adult book group. Her modeling illustrates a reader's thinking process—how to disagree with a statement, identify turning points, and look for connections to other parts of the book.

Bookmarks   Bookmarks provide support for both reading and gathering information. As they read, students in Lori Scobie's class use the bookmark to record interesting or puzzling words they encounter and to write questions for their group (Figure 5.6). Janine King's sixth graders use a different bookmark to keep track of the number of pages each group agrees to read. For the second and third graders in Mary Lou Laprade's class, a bookmark serves as a place to record interesting ideas or facts worth discussing.

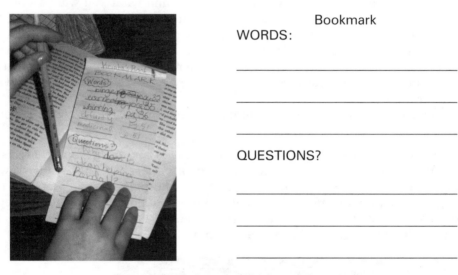

Figure 5.6 Bookmark: Words and Questions

Golden Lines   Lori Scobie encourages her students to find powerful quotes to share in their groups (Figure 5.7). These "golden lines" automatically provide interesting discussion material. Many students find it much easier to select something the author said than to come up with their own reactions. Therefore, Golden Lines are an easy and effective strategy for gathering information to discuss. The Golden Lines form is very simple to prepare; you can just staple a lined piece of paper into students' response journals for this purpose.

Discussion Logs   As you can see from the examples in Figures 5.8 and 5.9, discussion logs are a more structured way to prompt students to collect quotes, questions, and interesting words. Some teachers find that having students write down what they want to share in the discussion helps everyone participate more fully—and be more accountable. The log provides just enough space for a quick notation; it differs from a journal, whose purpose is more extended and reflective response.

When she first began literature circles, Kirstin Gerhold collected the discussion log in Figure 5.8 to see what students were sharing when she was not able to observe

GOLDEN LINES

"As M'ma gasped, the children flung themselves at her and she clasped them in her arms, hugging them."

p. 30
Journey to Jo'burg
by Beverly Naidoo

Figure 5.7 Golden Lines

the group. She also used the log to compare what students wrote with what she observed in the discussion. Notice how the log asks students for the same information as that gathered by the "quote and question" strategy described earlier in this chapter.

Some teachers ask students to list unfamiliar words in their discussion logs. Asking students to find words they don't know can result in lists overflowing (their books were challenging for them) or empty (they didn't want to admit that there were words they didn't know). Kirstin's version of the log provides a way for students to collect "wonder words"—a term coined by second grade teacher Gordon Kelly for words his students wondered about. This became the place for Kirstin's students to list unusual or descriptive words that they encountered and wished to discuss.

Literature Circles Discussion Log

Title and Author: _____

For Discussion Date: _____

Reading Assignment: _____

A part that I would like to share with my group:
(Write the first and last word and the page number.) _____
_____

One question that I have about the reading: _____
_____

Wonder Words: Write three words from your reading that you wonder about and want to talk about with your group.

_____   _____   _____

Figure 5.8 Discussion Log

When Lori Scobie first started literature circles, she adapted a form that she picked up at a workshop (Figure 5.9). Discovering this form was a relief to Lori; she felt her students needed the type of support such a form provides. Notice how this form asks students to do some thinking and writing as they read and prepare for the discussion. It blends the concept of discussion prompts with a simple management structure ("Are You Ready?").

Literature Response Log

Name_____ Pages _____ Date _____

Title _____ Author _____

Journal Response

_____

_____

_____

Points for Discussion

I'd like to talk to my group about . . . I'd like to ask them . . . I wonder why . . . It was interesting that/when . . .

_____

_____

_____

Are You Ready?

__ I finished my assigned reading   __ I completed my response
__ I dated and labeled my responses __ I marked the parts I
__ I put my best effort into my work   wanted to share

Figure 5.9 Literature Response Log

Many teachers find, as Lori did, that forms are helpful in the very beginning. However, Lori quickly realized that this form didn't work for her students because they tended to read directly from the form instead of using it as a prompt for real conversation. At that point, Lori abandoned discussion forms altogether and relied on students' bookmarks, Golden Lines, and journals.

Our recurring advice is this: Be selective about the tools and strategies that you offer students. If juggling all the pieces—bookmarks, Post-it Notes, discussion logs—becomes students' focus, they may never experience the real nature of an engaging discussion.

Learning to Participate in a Discussion

There's no getting around it: Learning to participate as an effective listener and contributor during discussions challenges students at all levels. This is understandable given the demanding nature of social interactions. If your discussions are student led with you as an observer—or not even there much of the time—the challenge increases. Managing their own interactions may be new for your students. At times, we all may have difficulty listening well to others and contributing our own ideas. Finding meaningful things to say about what they've read, as well as participating as an active member of the discussion, requires skills that many students have not yet developed. Therefore, the time and effort you invest in teaching, practicing, and debriefing the process of discussion will pay crucial dividends.

Teach the Process   You may need to teach your students how to talk with others about books in a way that invites everyone's participation and that builds a shared understanding of the book.

First, a key consideration. Paradoxical as it may seem, all of the teachers we work with did not teach a process of effective discussion until *after* their students had some experience. During Lori Scobie's first round of literature circles, for example, her focus was on the basic structure—and survival—not yet on rich discussion. She knew her students needed to "jump in" before they would be able to think more deeply about the challenges of discussion. Because Lori allowed her students to try discussions first, they experienced those challenges first hand. When she was ready to teach them how to discuss more effectively, they were ready to learn. They had a need to know.

Here are some steps teachers and students take as they learn the process of discussion:

Brainstorm: What works and what doesn't in a discussion? As with other aspects of literature circles, the *most* effective way to identify what works and what doesn't in discussions is to involve your students and let them tell you. The *least* effective way is for you to tell them. Why? For one thing, if they have tried discussions in literature circles or in any other setting in your classroom, your students already know what works and what doesn't. But more importantly, you can engender ownership and engagement directly by allowing your students to develop their own guidelines and ground rules.

We offer two examples of brainstorming in preparation for literature circle discussions. The first is a simple strategy that works well in primary classrooms; the second is a more elaborate way to guide students to understand the elements of good discussion in depth.

- *Brainstorming based on general literary experiences.* To make discussion easier for her first grade students, Vicki Yousoofian incorporated the same ground rules that guided all types of interactions with books in her classroom. Before she introduced literature circles, she and her students brainstormed answers to the question, "How do we act when we listen to or discuss a story?" In that initial session, the class developed the first guideline: "Listen to each other and the teacher." The class gradually added others: "Accept each others ideas," "Ask questions," Don't interrupt." By the time Vicki introduced literature circles in November, her students were already familiar with and able to use these basic guidelines.

- *Brainstorming based on "immersion" experiences.* Lori Scobie knew that her fourth graders would have far greater buy-in for discussion guidelines if they could see a real need for them. She believed that immersing her students in a discussion was the fastest way for them to learn what guidelines they needed. She initiated a brainstorming session one day following a short literature circle discussion. After students had met for about ten minutes, Lori gathered everyone in the front of the room where they conduct their class meetings. Writing their responses on a large piece of chart paper, Lori asked them what they liked about meeting in groups for literature circles. Here's what they said:

> *Sharing feelings about the book.*
> *We shared if we liked the book or not.*
> *We got to talk about different parts of the book.*

When she made another column on the chart, "How can we improve?" many hands went up:

> *Some people can't read as fast as others*
> *Not interrupting*
> *Trying not to goof around*
> *Working together*
> *Getting started right away*
> *Talking more; some talked a lot and some didn't talk much*

Develop classroom guidelines and ground rules for discussion. After Lori's students identified the benefits and challenges of discussions, she explained that it was time for them to develop guidelines. Lori said, "I like 'guideline' better than 'rule' because it says this is what we've agreed to work toward. Our guidelines will help us make our discussions as productive as they can be."

Pointing to each comment on the chart, Lori asked for a positive way to phrase it. For example, she began with the statement, "Some people can't read as fast as others." Carolyn suggested that they needed a guideline about not reading ahead, since those who knew what had happened sometimes told—spoiling it for those who hadn't read as far. Several students agreed that this was a big problem. Lori asked, "Since this seems to be a real concern, is there a positive statement we can make for this guideline?" Mobi offered, "There will be no reading ahead." Ashley then pointed out that some students have a hard time reading as fast as others. The class shaped another guideline: "Read during silent reading to catch up." After about 20 minutes of negotiation, the guidelines list was finished.

Figure 5.10 presents the guidelines for Lori's classroom. As you can see, the list is short. Lori kept the number of items limited to those she felt were most important. Although she may have had additional guidelines in mind, she was willing to begin with these—they covered everything that was crucial.

Identify the elements of effective discussion. Kirstin Gerhold wanted her fifth graders to understand the elements of good discussion. For example, she wasn't sure they really knew what being an "active listener" meant. Kristin discussed with her students what each element of discussion "looks like" and "sounds like" using the chart in Figure 5.11.

First, Kirstin presented the grid with just the "Discussion Elements" column filled in. She guided her students to generate specific examples of what they would see and hear when each aspect of discussion worked smoothly. Therefore, the examples in the "Looks Like" and "Sounds Like" columns are written in the students' words. After the

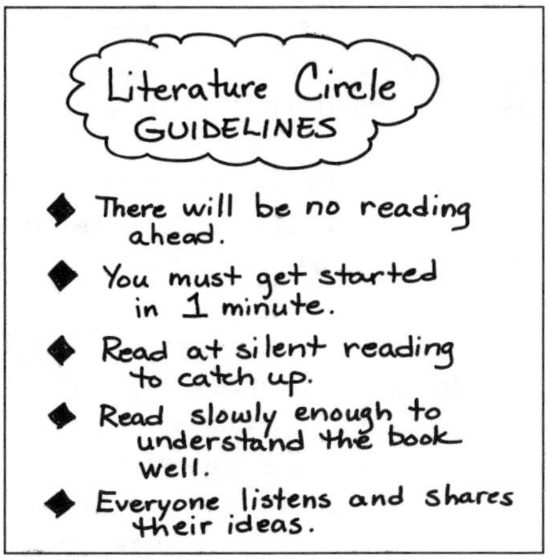

> Literature Circle
> GUIDELINES
>
> ◆ There will be no reading
>   ahead.
> ◆ You must get started
>   in 1 minute.
> ◆ Read at silent reading
>   to catch up.
> ◆ Read slowly enough to
>   understand the book
>   well.
> ◆ Everyone listens and shares
>   their ideas.

Figure 5.10
Student-Generated Guidelines

Discussion Elements	Looks Like	Sounds Like
Focused on Discussion Body posture Eye contact	*Eyes on speaker* *Hands empty* *Sit up* *Mind is focused* *Face speaker*	*Speaker's voice only* *Paying attention* *Appropriate responses* *Voices low* *One voice at a time*
Active Participation Respond to ideas Share feelings	*Eyes on speaker* *Hands to yourself* *Hands empty* *Talking one at a time* *Head nodding*	*Appropriate responses* *Follow off others' ideas* *Nice comments* *Positive attitudes*
Asking Questions for Clarification	*Listening* *Hands empty*	*Positive, nice questions* *Polite answers*
Piggybacking Off Others' Ideas	*Listening* *Paying attention*	*Positive, nice talking* *Wait for people to finish*
Disagreeing Constructively	*Look at the speaker* *Nice face, nice looks*	*Polite responses* *Let people finish talking* *Quiet voices* *No put downs*
Active Listening	*Paying attention* *Hands empty* *Looking at the speaker*	*Quiet* *Speaker's voice only*
Taking Turns to Let Others Speak	*One person talking* *Attention on the speaker*	*One voice*
Supporting Opinions with Evidence	*Use the book and form* *Be prepared*	*Piggybacking off others* *Help others find evidence* *One voice* *Let people finish talking*
Encouraging Others	*Prompt people to share* *Ask probing questions*	*Positive responses* *Appropriate responses*

Figure 5.11 Discussion Etiquette

entire grid was complete, Kirstin made copies for each student's response journal and a large sample as a classroom poster. During the early literature circle discussions, Kirstin's students often referred to the grid. Kirstin also used the grid during discussion debriefings (described later).

Your students may need fewer discussion elements to contend with in the early rounds of literature circles; they may also need different descriptors. If you choose to follow Kirstin's example, we suggest that you modify her process to fit what will work in your classroom.

"Fishbowl"—Model effective discussion. Perhaps the most powerful way for students to understand what goes into a good discussion is to observe one in action. If you have students in your classroom—or colleagues in other classrooms—who are discussion veterans, perhaps they can be models. Several of Janine King's sixth graders had participated in literature circles the year before. She used a common cooperative learning technique—a "fishbowl"—to model good discussion strategies for the rest of her class. Just as Lori did with the brainstorming session, Janine presented a discussion model after students had experienced one literature circle cycle with *Roll of Thunder, Hear My Cry* (Taylor, 1976). That way, she knew her students had a frame of reference to understand what they would see—and they had a clear need to know. Janine invited five students with strong discussion skills to participate in the demonstration. She asked each to re-read the last chapter and prepare a "quote and question" (discussed earlier in this chapter). For the demonstration, the group gathered chairs in a circle at the front of the room and began to talk. Although understandably self-conscious at first, the students quickly forgot the audience and engaged in an interesting discussion of the book's ending. Afterward, Janine asked, "What did you notice as you watched this discussion?" This generated a flood of responses. Because the discussion had taken place right in front of them, the students had no trouble picking out what worked. Janine's class generated the same kind of list as Lori's fourth graders did—and from their list grew the guidelines that they used for the rest of the year. Janine says the fishbowl technique made a big difference in her students' understanding of how to discuss: "That was the big toe in the water for us before we put the whole foot in."

A fishbowl demonstration can be highly effective even if your students have little prior experience to draw on. In this case, the participants may offer a more authentic demonstration that gives you lots of material on which to comment. Lori Scobie tried this during her first literature circle on *Dear Mr. Henshaw* (Cleary, 1983), and here's how it went:

Volunteers gathered in front of the room with their books and their journals. Carolyn jumped in first. "This is what I noticed," she said, speaking softly. "I liked where it showed the boy's journal and I wondered why he wrote to Mr. Henshaw." Jarrett, sitting next to her, said, "Well, I didn't hear Carolyn's question, but this is what I wrote . . ."

Lori stepped in. "This is the hard part," she told them and talked about responding to each other rather than just going on to the next person. She asked Carolyn to read her journal entry again and this time Derrick made a comment about what she said. Jarrett added, "I agree with Carolyn about that. I was wondering why he wrote to Mr. Henshaw, too."

This was what Lori was looking for. "Wow," she said, "I just noticed so many fabulous things. No one raised their hands to talk. They just knew when to talk. You want to have it like when you're at the dinner table. I also noticed that people listened and added something new. They were listening *and* preparing to talk at the same time." By drawing attention to a few specifics, Lori helped her students get a feel for good conversation.

Practice and Debrief   Students of all ages will need lots of practice with discussion before it begins to take off. This may be one of the *few* certainties about literature circle discussions. Therefore, we encourage you to keep your expectations for discussion realistic. We have found that students become more adept at these conversations gradually. This is helped when teachers take time to debrief the discussions by drawing students together afterward and reviewing what went well and what is still challenging. Every teacher who participated in this book will tell you that the cycle of practice and debriefing is where they begin to see growth. Here are some things to keep in mind:

Keep the debriefing short and focused. A debriefing session does not need to take a lot of time in order to be effective. Lori Scobie conducts whole-class debriefings for five to ten minutes after the groups have discussed. Vicki Yousoofian's first graders absorb a few helpful tips in quick debriefings immediately after their discussion.

Start simply. Ask your students a couple of simple questions: "What worked well today?" and "What do we still need to work on?" Lori does this while standing in front of the literature circle guidelines chart (see Figure 5.10). If an issue comes up that seems to be important, she may add another guideline to the list.

Use debriefing to teach specific strategies students can use in their next discussion. Debriefing offers an excellent way to help students become conscious of what works and what doesn't in a discussion. You can achieve this best when students understand specifics. As an example, listen to what Janine King told one group as she debriefed their discussion: "You had two parts to your discussion today—predictions and questions. One generated more discussion. Which was that?" One student said, "Our questions." When Janine asked the group why they thought that was true, someone said, "When you give your prediction, you can't really argue with that. It's their prediction." Janine built on that understanding: "When you're talking about something that's more of a statement, what could help the discussion?" Here's what the students suggested:

> *"Say your prediction, then ask, 'What do you think of that?'"*
> *"Ask, 'What do you think might happen later in the book?'"*
> *"Say, 'That's what I thought, too. Do you have any thoughts?'"*

Through this debriefing, students demonstrated that they know *what* goes into an effective discussion, and they're working on the *how*. Janine summed it up for them: "When someone makes a prediction and tells why, then you can piggyback on that other person's prediction." Students came away with specific strategies to apply right away in their next discussion.

Guide Students' Self-Reflection

Begin with reflections in response journals. The response journal provides a good place for student self-reflection on discussions. Useful prompts include, "What went well in your discussion today?" "What was something that you did to help the discussion go smoothly?" "What will you work on for next time?" In a journal entry, one of Mary Lou Laprade's third graders wrote: "Yesterday, I think that the book club discussion went pretty good because we all were good listeners and we all participated. We kept the discussion going and we all had a lot of fun." Journal entry reflections give you helpful assessment information about your students' ability to identify and articulate the elements of effective discussion.

Introduce a few forms to guide reflection. You can also use forms and handouts for debriefing, such as the form (Figure 5.12) developed by first grade teacher Megan Sloan (1995).

Literature Circle Evaluation

Name _____ Date _____

Literature Circle Group _____

Book_____

WHAT THINGS DID YOUR GROUP DO VERY WELL TODAY?

___ started in 1 minute   ___ cooperation
___ read and follow along   ___ discussion

WHAT THINGS ARE GOING REALLY WELL IN YOUR DISCUSSIONS?

___ listening to others   ___ asking questions
___ everyone is sharing   ___ supporting ideas
___ predicting what will happen next   ___ relating to own lives
___ relating to other books or characters

Figure 5.12 Discussion Evaluation Form

When you're ready for other examples, you will find a variety of debriefing forms and processes in Bonnie Campbell Hill's chapter on assessment and evaluation in *Literature Circles and Response* (1995). As with everything else about literature circles, you'll gradually find what works best for you and your students.

Assessing and Evaluating Discussions

Literature circle discussions provide a realistic and valuable opportunity to learn about students' literacy strengths and challenges, as well as their ability to talk with one another about books. There are many ways to collect and analyze assessment information generated by the discussions. What we offer here are some "getting started" processes that work well in the early stages of literature circles. Basic discussion assessment includes observations you make as you listen in on (or drop into) discussions and students' self-reflections. One form of assessment can inform and verify the other.

Anecdotal Notes

Many teachers find value in taking time to make short, specific anecdotal notes as they listen in on the discussion. For example, Janine King uses anecdotal notes to gather assessment information as she observes her sixth graders' discussions (see Figure 3.7).

These notes do not need to be elaborate. You can record different types of observations: Strategies you notice students using as they re-read their books for the discussion, types of thinking students demonstrate in the discussion, actions students take (or fail to take) that affect the discussion. *What* you record is limited only by your goals. When new to literature circles, however, most teachers keep their anecdotal notes limited. It is challenging to manage all of the components of literature circles *and* make specific observations about what students are learning. Therefore, we offer these two suggestions: Use Post-it Notes and limit the focus of your observations.

For example, Vicki Yousoofian made a checklist of things she wanted to look for in children's discussions and written response (Figure 5.13). She used Post-it Notes, writing each child's name and the date, to record key ideas that students shared. Vicki developed focus lessons based on what she observed in the discussions and response journals. Such a manageable system helped her track students' growth in reading and writing strategies.

Look for . . .	Post-it Notes . . .	
Asking questions	Emily R. ²/₂₆ word choice "plomp" asked a question	Patrick H. ²/₂₆ Connected to family
Listening actively		
Thoughtful response		
Predicting		
Retelling -- main idea and supporting details	Brett 2/26 black kb-- Connected	Emily G ²/₂₆ smell dust misty smells
Supporting ideas and opinions with text		
Elements of literature (plot, setting, etc.)	JC 2/26 "get thirsty while reading"	Tat 2/26 Connect to other books
Making personal connections		
Connectioning to other books		

Figure 5.13
Checklist and Post-it Notes
for Anecdotal Observations

Vicki's remarks on the Post-it Notes included observations about individual children's comments. For example, on one Post-it Note Vicki wrote, "Emily R.: Word choice = 'plomp'; asked a question." Another recorded, "Patrick: Connected to family." These short, but specific, notes later helped Vicki determine what kinds of responses her first graders made to the story.

You will devise your own note-making system. The main point is this: Find a way to record what you observe as students discuss and write so that you have an idea of the kinds of thinking they demonstrate.

Self-Reflection

Basic and informative self-reflection is also very easy: Ask students to tell you (or write in their journals) what worked well for them during the discussion and what was difficult. As an extension of this idea, Lori Scobie developed a form (Figure 5.14) to help students reflect on their participation in discussions. In the form, you will see how Lori incorporated her students' discussion guidelines (see Figure 5.10). This serves two purposes: To inform Lori and her students about their participation in discussions and to remind students to pay attention to the guidelines they constructed.

Name: _____

Date: _____

1 = nope, 2 = sort of, 3 = OK, 4 = good, 5 = WOW!

PREPARATION

I read up to page ___ and not ahead.	1 2 3 4 5
If I needed to catch up I took the responsibility to read at home, recess or silent reading.	1 2 3 4 5
I completed my journal entry with things to share.	1 2 3 4 5
I wrote new words and interesting pages on my bookmark ahead of time.	1 2 3 4 5

CIRCLE TIME:

I helped my group get started in **ONE** minute.	1 2 3 4 5
I helped keep the noise level in class low.	1 2 3 4 5
I was an active listener.	1 2 3 4 5
I stayed on task and didn't goof around.	1 2 3 4 5
I shared something with my group. How many things? _____	1 2 3 4 5
I responded to someone else's comment. How many times? _____	1 2 3 4 5

Figure 5.14 Discussion Rating Form Based on Student-Generated Criteria

Mary Lou Laprade developed a rubric for literature circles ("book clubs" in her classroom) which incorporated criteria for all aspects of the process—from being prepared to participating in the discussion. She introduced this rubric (Figure 5.15) to her second and third graders and asked them to rate their own participation in the discussion.

Figure 5.15
Rubric for "Book Clubs"

Book Clubs

0	1	2	3
• Not prepared	• Read a little bit	• Read all assigned pages	• Read all assigned pages
• Hasn't read book	• Not prepared to discuss	• Minimal amount of assigned writing	• Prepared to discuss
• Doesn't bring materials	• Hasn't done assigned writing	• Little participation in group discussion	• Eager to share
• Does not use good listening skills	• Does not use good listening skills	• Uses good listening skills most of the time	• Uses good listening skills
			• Good effort on written assignment

Some Final Thoughts on Discussion

Remember that learning to discuss takes time and energy. That discovery can be disheartening, but it's worth the effort to make conversations work. Janine King says, "You know, we started the discussions and they were fantastic—but there were times when they weren't. You can't just say, 'Oh, they're working great, I've got that done, and I can move on to other things.' You have to keep going back and making sure they stay great. You have to keep working at it."

What is worth worrying about?

- Set a clear purpose for discussion.

- Carefully and deliberately teach all facets of discussion: Deciding what to talk about, finding and collecting information to share, taking part in the discussion.

- Involve your students in setting guidelines and ground rules.

- Debrief discussions regularly in order to refine guidelines and build strategies.

- Maintain realistic expectations—for yourself and for your students.

- Establish ways to move students beyond "I like the book."

- Use tools sparingly—prompts, forms, questions.

What is worth letting go?

- The expectation that every discussion will soar. Good conversations are part art and part magic and develop with time and experience.

- The idea that you must sit in on every discussion . . . or that your students must always discuss independently.

- The notion that there exists a "perfect" discussion; conversations have lives of their own—no two will ever be alike.

Common Questions About Discussion

How much time should a discussion take?

Primary grade students may say what they have to say in 5 to 10 minutes. That may also be true for intermediate grade students, especially when they are just learning the process of discussion. You will get a feel for this as you and your students gain more experience.

Should I have parent facilitators for each group?

Parents—and other volunteers—can help you facilitate discussions *if* they understand their role. Just as you are neither the questioner nor the focus of students' attention—the adult facilitator must take a guiding-but-not-dominating stance. This may not be easy for parents who haven't participated in an adult book group. You may need to provide guidelines for facilitators, with such information as example questions to prompt discussion and how to get a flagging discussion going again.

What should I expect from their discussions? How can I foster quality discussions?

You may need to be patient with yourself and with your students as you figure out literature circles together. Listening to others, finding the place and time to interject your own ideas, forming what you want to say—these skills all take time to develop. In the beginning, your students' discussions may be quite short and limited. For example, Kirstin Gerhold's students first started their discussions with questions they had about the chapter. They took turns going around the group reading the questions—but nobody answered or reacted to the questions. It was a start. As Kirstin observed, debriefed with the whole class following discussions, and helped them practice new strategies, her students *gradually* became more adept at talking *as well as* interacting with one another.

What do I do when discussions go off track or go flat?

First of all, this will happen, and it doesn't mean that literature circles have failed. Even the most engaging conversations lose their zest. It's part of the nature of discussions. Therefore, solve it with those most closely involved—your students. Talk about ways to get a flagging discussion back in gear, and ask them to come up with some suggestions. Lori Scobie's students created just such a chart when this happened to them (Figure 5.16).

Figure 5.16
How to Keep a Discussion Going

Do students have to have roles?

Some teachers feel more comfortable starting out with a limited number of roles such as facilitator and recorder that may be familiar to students from cooperative learning activities. However, other teachers and students do not see a need for them. Whether you choose to use student roles in discussion will depend—as everything does—on experience and style. If you find that roles would be helpful for you, we recommend the clear descriptions in Chapter 5 of Harvey Daniels' book, *Literature Circles: Voice and Choice in the Student-Centered Classroom* (1994). We have seen some drawbacks to using roles: In some cases, the roles themselves take precedence over the conversation. Nearly all of the teachers we know who used roles early in the process abandoned them after awhile.

We've brainstormed a list of things to talk about, and still the groups sometimes just sit there and look at each other—or at me! What can I do to help them find grist for the conversation without dictating what they'll discuss?

This is one of the challenges of discussion and well worth working with your students to solve. As your students learn how to discuss, you may need to guide them more than you want to. First, let them in on the problem and ask them to help you with a solution. Janine King did this with her sixth graders. As a bridge to completely student-centered conversations, she gave the groups an open-ended focus, such as talking about their favorite character or connecting to their own lives.

What if one student dominates or doesn't participate?

Your students will naturally vary in their experiences, interests, and abilities within literature circles—just as they do in all aspects of your classroom. We have found that when students feel a real sense of ownership within their groups—having worked together to generate guidelines, having choice in what they discuss, negotiating with you and with their peers about how much to read at a time—they begin to manage themselves more effectively. Peer pressure can be positive and powerful.

In addition, if you debrief the discussions on a regular basis, students will have the chance to talk about what is working and what is getting in the way. Debriefing identifies those challenges that need attention. You may need a focus lesson or two to help all group members work on the skill of drawing each other into the conversation. They can brainstorm and practice finding invitations such as, "What do you think?" When that works, the less-forceful students don't have to depend on it being their "turn" to talk and can get into the discussion.

How about the student who comes to the group unprepared?

Peers can be very effective in this case, as well. When this happened in Janine King's classroom, the groups let her know. She would tell the student, "Well, you can sit and listen . . . but you probably won't have much to say today." She felt that sitting with the group was still a good use of the student's time, since he or she could gain a lot from listening in on the discussion. "But," she says, "the group would be disgusted and they'd let the student know. They found out pretty quickly that it's no fun to discuss something you haven't read. I didn't ever have to do anything about it—the group's reaction took care of everything. It only happened a few times."

What if one student reads ahead and gives away the exciting parts?

This is a difficult issue for many readers—even adults. It can be painful to make yourself stop reading just when the action kicks in. Janine King had this experience, too. Her sixth graders took the I-Will-Not-Read-Ahead Oath before every literature circle. When someone slipped and revealed something others hadn't yet encountered in their books, the group censure took care of it. Janine talked with her students about alternatives to reading ahead, such as finding other books to read when they had finished the sections their group had agreed on. She says, "It gets to the point where you don't even have to tell them why it's important not to spill the beans. Once they've experienced it in their group, they know."

Here are two strategies that work for other teachers whose students have a hard time not reading ahead and/or giving anything away:

- Before students discuss, suggest that they re-read the last page of the section they will discuss. Refreshing their memory about what was happening in the "legal" sections can be a big help.

- Ask students to place a rubber band around the portion of the book that they haven't yet read. This physical barrier can be a good reminder about how far the group has agreed to read.

What do I do with my challenged readers? I really want them to take part in the discussions, but they can't keep up with the reading.

Because discussion helps children construct meaning collaboratively, it can be a very powerful support for those students who struggle with reading. The key is to find ways for them to understand what the book is saying so that they *can* benefit from and contribute to the discussion.

Guiding challenged readers may include some of these strategies presented in Chapter 3: Reading the book ahead of time with resource teachers or other specialists, partner reading the book with a classmate, and/or listening to the book on tape as they read along.

Lori Scobie had several fourth graders who spent part of their day outside of her classroom working with the ESL or resource room teachers. Although challenged by the literature circle reading, they had insightful ideas and experiences to share in the discussions. She knew that they would contribute to literature circles as well as benefit from the collaboration with others. Therefore, she arranged for the students to read their literature circle books during instructional time with specialists. She also paired her challenged readers with classmates for shared reading. Because of this additional support, these students participated as fully as others who read more easily.

Post-it Notes are a great idea, but I can't afford to buy them for my classroom—what do other teachers do?

Although Post-it Notes are great for marking passages to share, you don't have to use them. Marking passages with a paper clip can be as effective. Simple bookmarks—either plain paper or photocopied forms discussed in this chapter—also work well. Some teachers use scraps of recycled paper for students' questions, quotes, "discussible" words. In addition, Lori Scobie's "Golden Lines" requires just a sheet of paper—but is extremely effective in helping students search the text for something to talk about.

There are also some less-costly ways to use Post-it Notes. One teacher we know gives her students one pack at the beginning of the year and tells them that this is it—when the pack is gone, they're on their own. She laughs when she says, "By about February, my students are marking their books with teeny scraps of those Post-its. They really make them last!" In other classrooms, families supply Post-it Notes as part of their child's regular school supplies.

Chapter 6

Response Journals

. . . their discussions were so rich, and then their journals were so lacking in depth, and the point is, we spent weeks learning how to have good discussions, and then I said, "Oh, go write in your journals." I never addressed how to make a good journal entry. . . . you have to teach it . . . that point came through strongly.

—Janine King, sixth grade teacher

While it feels natural to talk about books, the feeling sometimes vanishes when we're asked to write or sketch our response. In the world outside of school and when we read for personal reasons, we rarely interrupt our reading flow to write out questions, explain why we think the main character is a bully, or sketch a vivid scene. And yet, when we do pause during reading, and turn to paper, pen, or crayon in the process, we create new possibility as readers. We also end up with something tangible, something easier to return to than talk. These tangible pieces become valuable to guide our discussions and useful to track what's happening as we read.

This chapter expands journals beyond spiral notebooks and response beyond chapter summaries or predictions of a character's fate. Rather, it aims to develop how during-reading response moves beyond talk to include other response forms. It also describes ways to teach and evaluate such responses. Our suggestions about using journals with literature circles develop from the process outlined in Figure 6.1.

Making Response Journals Work

Clarify purposes for journals—for yourself and for your students
Help students know what to focus on in their journals
- Use Open-Ended Prompts
- Use Questions That Come Up in Discussions
- Use Questions From Outside Resources
- Consider Other Forms of Response
- Try Sketching and Drawing

Recognize how and why responses change over time

Teach students how to write a journal entry
- Introduce
- Demonstrate
- Practice
- Debrief, reflect, assess

Figure 6.1 Making Response Journals Work

Clarify Your Purposes for Response Journals

Think of response journals as thinking tools. Many writers keep a notebook or journal to capture and try out new ideas. Their journals offer a place to explore and perform without fear of criticism and prior to final draft commitment. Readers also deserve a place for tentative exploration. Journals and notebooks support the writing *and* reading process. Both processes involve interpretation and creation and both require active engagement. When used during literature circles, response journals can help readers remember what they've read, offer a place to raise questions, and create interaction with characters, events, and issues. Such engagement occurs by indirectly slowing readers down long enough to think, respond, and interact. If your goal for literature circles is in-depth reading with readers taking a more active role, you'll find response journals a useful tool to support this.

Third grade teacher Mary Lou Laprade sees journal writing as an important part of literature circles in her classroom for many reasons. She aims for her students' reading response journals to:

- Use the writer's own language

- Allow the reader/writer to explore feelings

- Facilitate the transaction between the reader and the book

- Help the teacher develop insight into how the children are developing as readers

- Provide a place and space for readers to develop their responses to what they're reading

- Encourage children to make predictions

- Help children make connections to their own life or to other books they have read

- Give students a place to reflect on their literature circle meetings

Other teachers include reading response journals as a key component of literature circles for additional reasons. Kristen Gephart's second graders use reading response journals as:

- A place to "think" in writing/drawing about what he/she read.

- A place where a literary dialogue can happen between the student and me or the student and his/her peers.

- A place for readers to respond personally in preparation for discussion.

If you're just getting started with literature circles, your reasons to use response journals may not be as clearly defined as Mary Lou's or Kristen's. They will, however, become clearer the more you focus on what happens when you teach students how to think on paper. As with all components of literature circles, it may help to begin with a simple goal such as using response journals to support discussions. No matter your goal, there is great value when your students also know how and why journals are being kept.

Help Students Understand the Purpose of Response Journals

Most students need tangible reasons for keeping a response journal. They'll want to know *what* to write as well as *why* they're writing in the first place. What to write will be explained later in this chapter. Why they're writing is explained here.

One way to help students see the benefits of keeping a response journal is to help them understand that:

- You can use your journal during the discussion.

- Other people may listen to the ideas you've written in your journal.

- Your teacher will read and respond to your ideas.

The most obvious benefit from keeping a response journal is to support the direction of literature circle discussions. When journal responses are shared during discussions, the journal moves from being a personal repository of ideas, to the spark that ignites the discussion (see Chapter 5). And, when students are given an audience—their classmates as well as their teacher—they learn that their ideas have value.

Regardless of format or content, we've found it imperative that journals become more than something we assign because we need a literature circles grade. Students know the difference between assignments for their teacher's purposes and assignments for theirs. Often their effort reflects this knowledge. The sooner response journals are used during discussions, the better. When we read journals and write back to students—with words and not grades—we share the benefits, increase possibility for participation, and continue their thinking about the book.

Over time, as students try out new prompts, questions, and diverse response forms, they can also discover internal motivations to keep a journal. They'll learn how pausing during reading to write and sketch can help them understand, predict, wonder, discover, and extend interpretation. They may also learn how such work affects not only their reading, but also their writing. This doesn't usually occur right away, and probably never will, unless students experience what can happen when their ideas find an audience.

Help Students Understand How to Focus Their Journal Responses

Many students freeze when confronted by a blank piece of paper and the direction to "Respond to what you've just read." We need to help our students see what's possible to focus on in a journal response, and learn numerous ways to respond on paper. Introducing a few structured prompts and teaching students the strategies to use them effectively builds students' confidence as they grow into more sophisticated readers.

Use Open-Ended Prompts

Many of the teachers we work with use prompts and examples to teach what's possible as a reading response and to guide readers beyond common, but limited "I like it" or "I like the part . . ." responses. The list of prompts in Figure 6.2 works well for readers of all ages and abilities because they're open-ended and they do not elicit one specific answer. These may look very familiar if you have recently read Chapter 5, since the similar prompts serve to guide discussions as well as written responses.

Journal Prompts

I liked . . .

I noticed . . .

I wonder . . .

I felt _____ because . . .

I think . . .

This story makes me think of . . .

I wish . . .

If I were _____, I would . . .

When I . . .

I was surprised by . . .

Figure 6.2 Journal Prompts

We recommend using these prompts as you and your students begin with written response. You may find it most manageable when you:

- Introduce prompts one or two at a time.

- Demonstrate how you'd use the prompt in your own response.

- Invite students to try out the prompt.

Introduce One or Two Prompts at a Time One of the fastest ways to confuse students is to teach too much at once. Even something as simple as open-ended prompts becomes complex if the entire list is introduced on the same day. We recommend giving students a chance to learn how each prompt works, not with a "fill in the blank" mentality, but with thinking that includes ideas from the book and from the reader's life.

Many teachers begin with the prompt, "I wonder . . .", because it moves readers away from "I like it . . ." statements into a questioning stance. When such questioning takes place, ideas are introduced that other readers can react to and try to answer. Responses to this prompt remind us that young readers' curiosities are not always what adult readers anticipate (see Figure 6.3).

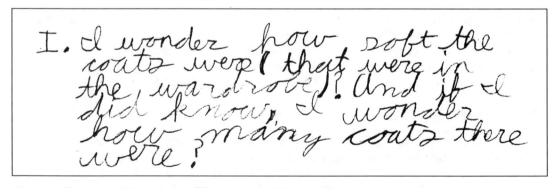

Figure 6.3 Response to *The Lion, the Witch, and the Wardrobe* (Lewis, 1994).

Start with one or two prompts, then gradually introduce others. As each prompt is introduced, write it onto chart paper, large enough to be visible to everyone in class. With one or two prompts introduced each week, the list grows over time, until it becomes a resource from which students can choose the response that best fits their book. Once all prompts have been taught, some teachers photocopy the list, then have students tape it inside the cover of their response journals. This provides an accessible reminder of what's possible when students are ready to make their own choices.

Demonstrate How You'd Use the Prompt in Your Own Response   The easiest way to teach students how to write responses from prompts is to demonstrate the process as they watch and listen. This can be done either as a whole class focus lesson or during a literature circle meeting. When writing your response in front of your students, use an overhead projector or chart paper, and talk through your thinking as you come up with ideas. Don't worry about crafting a perfect response. Instead, put your energy into teaching the process of thinking that results in a written response.

Many teachers use the book they're reading aloud to demonstrate written responses. When you do this, you guarantee more student interest and interaction since this is the book the whole class knows. You may want to write your entire response in front of your students, or you might want to start the response at home (or during recess) and elicit help from your students in finishing it. You may also want to use student responses as demonstrations. Make an overhead transparency of these responses and ask students to "show and tell" their process. As they learn how to talk about their response, you may need to guide their telling with some questions.

Invite Students to Try Out the Prompt   When we offer a demonstration, the focus is on teaching. To shift the focus to learning, we need to give students a chance to use what was taught. This is easily done by asking students to use the demonstrated prompt when they respond to their literature circles book. Once they do this, take time to talk through what happened. Read their responses. Let them share what they write with others. Provide time for questions, for more examples, and for ways to deepen the response with specifics from the book.

When you begin teaching from prompts, the going might seem slow and even unnatural. Remember, your goal is to nudge readers beyond "I like it" responses by providing other possibilities. Within a few weeks your students will acquire a menu of prompts from which to choose and strategies they can use to approach their journals with confidence and success.

Once writing prompts become familiar and useful, they may also become rote. When this happens, you need to shift from prompts to other response forms such as the suggestions that follow.

Use Questions that Come Up in Discussion

Mary Lou Laprade finds that discussions held during her third graders' literature circles serve to inspire ideas for future written responses. For example, when a student raises questions such as, "How did you feel while reading the book? Why?" or "What was the most exciting part or the strangest thing that happened?" Mary Lou encourages answers during their discussion. Then, she suggests that students use these questions to guide their next journal response.

Mary Lou teaches written response by showing students her own journal entries written from the prompts she introduced to the class and questions that came up in their discussions. She encourages her students to share their journals aloud so that she can ask questions and comment verbally. She does this to help her students learn how others respond and continue thinking about what they've read. In so doing, she also provides an audience and a purpose for the response journals.

How do you know what questions to ask? The best resource is in your own class-room. Listen carefully during literature circles discussions and during conversations about your read-aloud book. You can also gather questions as you overhear students talk about books they're reading independently. Natural book talk includes both statements and questions. Jotting down the questions you hear provides one of the best lists to use.

Use Questions from Outside Resources

There are numerous resources available to guide you in developing response questions. If you're interested in open-ended questions that focus on literary elements, there's a useful list in Anne Klein's chapter in *Literature Circles and Response* (Hill et al., 1995) and in Regie Routman's *Invitations* (1994, p. 107). If you'd like help with questions about literary devices, pages 118–119 in *Invitations* offers a good place to start.

We're aware there are a number of literature guides on the market for individual books. While these may provide questions you hadn't considered and suggest steps to use in teaching the book, the authors of these guides don't know your students and their transaction as readers. We caution you to be selective if you turn to outside guides. Choose questions that fit your students, most naturally extending the response they've already developed. We also caution you to introduce questions gradually and in ways that guide and support rather than overwhelm.

Consider Other Forms of Response

The possible ways to respond to what we read is endless. Just as overuse of prompts can become rote, guided questions can become stale without variety or consideration of how they fit readers and books. Prompts and questions can also limit ways of thinking about what is read. The following response forms offer variety and a new focus for during-reading response.

- *Diary Entries*   Choose an incident or event from your story that might cause one of the characters to respond in a journal. Taking the role of the character, explain what happened and how you felt about it. You might want to create journal entries for more than one day in your character's life. In Figure 6.4, a third grader writes about his day's adventure in the voice of *Stuart Little* (White, 1945).

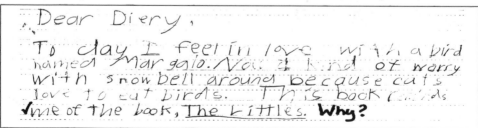

Figure 6.4 Journal Entries—Diary Entries

- *Cause/Effect Explanation* Find a place in your book where something happened as a result of an action taken by a character or by an event that occurred. On one side of your paper illustrate what you see as the cause. Write a brief explanation underneath. On the other side, illustrate the result and write your explanation of that. In Figure 6.5, a first grader explains an instance of cause and effect in *Ruby the Copycat* (Rathmann, 1991).

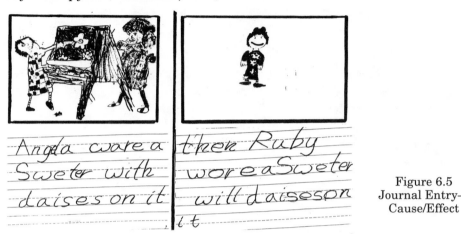

Figure 6.5
Journal Entry—
Cause/Effect

Letters Write a letter to a friend, to your literature circle group, to a character in your book, or to the author. Share your thoughts, questions, and feelings about the book so far. In Figure 6.6, a third grader identifies with the anxiety of moving away as she writes to the main character in *Aldo Applesauce* (Harwitz, 1979).

> Dear Aldo,
>   I know how you feel because I going to a new school. I am nevus butt I think you banld it very well I think I am going to do the same thing. I thought DeDe is funny in the story. You were very sportisve to De De when she had a prboum.
>   Your friend,
>   Sally

Figure 6.6 Journal Entry—Letter to a Character

Character Web   Draw a portrait of your selected character in the middle of your journal page. List 3 to 5 traits that describe that character; write these around the character's portrait. [Adaptation: Now find a specific passage from your book to support each trait. Copy that passage next to the trait. Be sure to list the page number.] Figure 6.7 shows an example from *The Story of Jackie Robinson: The Bravest Man in Baseball* (Davidson, 1988).

Figure 6.7
Journal Entry—Character Web

We realize this list is not the only one available to diversify during-reading responses. If you're interested in other journal response possibilities there are useful examples on pages 73 and 134–138 in *Literature Circles and Response* (Hill et al., 1995). When given a chance, students can also invent forms of response we won't find on any list. They're an excellent resource we mustn't forget to tap.

Most of the ideas listed above can also serve as extension projects culminating the ending of the book (see Chapter 8). Response occurs not just during the course of reading a book. It also isn't relegated to end-of-book thinking. We encourage you to experiment with these ideas during and after reading to discover how they may differ from thinking that prompts discussion and from ways of thinking that extend interpretation once the book's pieces have fallen into place.

Try Sketching and Drawing

One of the most natural ways for beginning readers and writers to respond is by sketching and drawing. While the physical act of writing a response is daunting to many young children, drawing a portrait of their favorite character or sketching a story's setting occurs without any "but I can't write yet" complaints. Inviting readers to draw or sketch as response is both valid and valuable . . . and it should be encouraged across the grades. There are times when words fail us. Drawing may help us discover some aspect of the book or story that mattered or that we're curious about. Thinking visually takes readers places that words may not. (See Figure 6.8.)

Using shape, design, image, and color as response tools offers students a way to create response. Some students find this a more accessible means of "talking" about their book. From their drawings come words—perhaps first through talk, then later accompanied by writing. Whether sketches stand alone or whether words accompany them, much can be discovered about a book from these diverse response forms.

Figure 6.8 Sketched
Journal Response

How and Why Response Journals Change Over Time

As noted in the chapter on discussion, experience with talk and the acquisition of tools and strategies to guide discussion makes a big difference in what our students do between the beginning and end of the year. The same holds true for response journals. In the beginning, it's often an "I like it" response that gets things started. Don't be discouraged by such responses. Instead, use them to build upon. Extend "I like it" into "I like it *because* . . ." showing readers how to return to the book or to their own lives for examples to support their opinion. In Figure 6.9, a sixth grader cites specific evidence to support her opinion of a favorite scene from *Roll of Thunder, Hear My Cry* (Taylor, 1976).

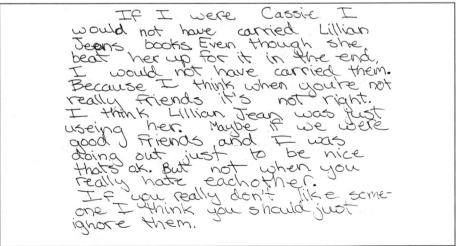

Figure 6.9 Journal Entry—Giving Evidence to Support an Opinion

At the beginning of the year, Janine King relies on open-ended prompts with her sixth graders. She isn't surprised when her students begin by writing short, surface responses. For example, to explain why he sketched a particular scene from *Family Pose* (Hughes, 1989), Matthew wrote, "I chose this scene because I thought it would be fun to draw a car accident."

Throughout the year, Janine demonstrates how to move from snapshot response to ones that include more evidence and deeper thought. As the year progresses, she notices how journal entries grow, as the entry about *Randall's Wall* (Fenner, 1991) shows in Figure 6.10. Janine knows these changes are the result of time spent teaching, demonstrating, and guiding students through the process.

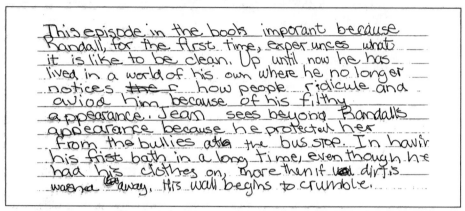

This episode in the book is important because Randall, for the first time, experiences what it is like to be clean. Up until now he has lived in a world of his own where he no longer notices the f how people ridicule and aviod him because of his filthy appearance. Jean sees beyond Randall's appearance because he protected her from the bullies at the bus stop. In havir his frist bath in a long time, even though he had his clothes on, more then if the dirt is washed away, His wall begins to crumble.

Figure 6.10 Journal Entry—Later in the Year

In addition to changes in response that are influenced by teaching, journal entries are also affected by students' maturity, by differences in skill, by interest in the book, and by personal experiences. Most of these influences are out of our control as teachers. Some take place as students develop, as they read more broadly, and as they respond not only to books but also to movies, television, art, and their world.

Teaching the Response Forms

Response forms are most effective when they're taught, rather than assigned. The format we recommend for teaching includes: Take time to introduce each response form. Then demonstrate—orally and visually—with strategies that show how to transfer in-your-head ideas onto paper. Encourage your students to try out the response form you've demonstrated. Then gather together again to debrief, reflect, and assess.

What does this look like in a classroom? It starts when the teacher sets a goal, usually one that's grown out of the work of the classroom. It continues with teaching and practice. Let's take a look into Lori Scobie's fourth grade classroom to view the process as it happens.

Teaching for In-Depth Journal Responses—One Teacher's Process

Lori introduced open-ended journal prompts at the beginning of the year and her students had many opportunities to use them. She noticed their journal responses were very short, some only one sentence long. From listening in during literature circles discussions, she knew her students had more to say about their books than was reflected in their writing. Knowing this, and seeking more thought-provoking responses, Lori articulated a goal: "I want to help students see the difference between a more in-depth journal response and the shorter reading log entries they use for their discussion." She set out to teach such responses using *Dear Mr. Henshaw* (Cleary, 1983), the novel the entire class was reading.

First, Lori gathered her students on the rug at the front of the room. Then she asked how they decide which passages to mark with Post-its in their literature circles book. Following this brief discussion, Lori mentioned that the pages they were scheduled to read that day included a part that startled her when she read it. In fact, she said, it included an incident that really made her think. Upon completing their reading, she would ask her students to do some "special writing" about that incident. With this in mind, Lori suggested they watch for that incident as they read. Then students moved away from the rug and began reading, some independently and others with partners.

After time to read, Lori gathered her students back together and showed them two transparencies. One was created to resemble their literature response log form (see Figure 5.9), while the other looked like a piece of notebook paper. Lori spoke about the small amount of writing space available on the reading log and reminded her students of the purpose of the log entries (to raise a question, to jot down a quick response). Then she started to write her journal response onto that small space. After one or two sentences she ran out of room. In fact, there was no room to offer much detail or explanation. Lori pointed this out to her students. As Josh, commented, "It's like a dictionary. It gives just a brief bit of detail." Lori agreed, pointing out how brief bits of writing were fine to prompt discussions, which fit the reading log's purpose. But, she told her students, readers need a place to write when there's more to say. As Lori placed the notebook paper transparency on the overhead projector she said,

> This gives me lots more room to say what I want. But it's also kind of intimidating. How do I begin? I might want to look up here at the journal starters (she pointed to the chart of journal prompts at the front of the room) to find something that helps me get started. 'I felt . . .'—that's exactly what I want because what I read today hit me right here (she points to her heart). I need all this space to write about my feelings in this part of the book.

Before sending her students back to their desks to write, Lori suggested they take a quick look at the places they'd marked for discussion, especially those that reflected how they were shocked, startled, or even surprised by the reading. Then she suggested they use those as their journal entry starting points.

What Lori provided were beginnings steps, with a useful tip, to guide her students' response writings. The result was similar to what happens when your own students try something new. Some of the students' entries were insightful, while others included strings of "I liked . . .", "I noticed . . .", "I felt . . ." statements. Carolyn's entry started with, "I felt that Leigh is in a web that's sticky with trouble." As we all keep discovering, students need plenty of support to begin writing more. They also need concrete ways of seeing how response entries differ from the short writings used on Post-its and in reading discussion logs.

There's nothing magical – or even extraordinary – about the decisions Lori made to *begin* teaching thoughtful response writing. What is important to consider is how her focus lesson grew out of her students' demonstrated needs and what Lori did to show another way to approach response writing. One lesson won't be enough, but it'll be a start.

Assessing and Evaluating Journal Responses

Journal responses offer valuable information to learn about students' interests and curiosities. In addition, most journal entries—especially if viewed over time—provide evidence of students' strengths, needs, and growth as readers and writers. As with the chapter on discussion, what we offer here are a few suggestions to get you started assessing and evaluating written and extended response. The caution is still to use these selectively and without feeling you need to do everything we suggest, certainly not at the beginning.

Rubrics

What rubrics offer are criteria and the belief that there are different stages or levels of what is acceptable or worthy. When such criteria are shared with students, expectations becomes overt, something useful when talking about and guiding whatever is being learned.

The most useful criteria are those developed in collaboration with students. They begin to gain a sense of what is valued as they closely examine the differences between journal entries with different ratings. They also benefit as they create the language used for each criterion.

Mary Lou Laprade developed a rubric for her third graders' journal responses with assistance from her students (Figure 6.11). First she asked the class to brainstorm a list of topics and qualities that result in a "good journal entry." As students called out ideas, Mary Lou wrote them onto chart paper. Later that day she reviewed the list, combining similar ideas and organizing them into related topics. As she did this, she took care to include language her students used and could understand and she listed qualities of writing and drawing that made sense to her students ("Has incomplete drawings" and "The illustrations are complete and add meaning and interest."). Because Mary Lou teaches her students to include both words and illustrations in their journal entries, both are assessed by the rubric. As she teaches new prompts and offers focus lessons on using specifics to support ideas, her rubric will change to include these new expectations. But, she begins with what she can expect, and that grows out of what's been taught and learned.

Mary Lou introduced the rubric for journal entries (Figure 6.11) in a focus lesson. She suggested that students use the rubric components as a guide for their writing. In this way Mary Lou developed students' conscious sense of the qualities for a "good" journal entry. Later in the year her students used the rubric to self-evaluate one journal entry from a literature circle unit. They reread every journal entry from that unit, then chose one entry to evaluate. This entry and the accompanying rubric became part of their portfolio.

You might find it helpful to borrow Mary Lou's rubric as the starting place with your students. Invite your students to select a journal response they consider "good" or

---

Rubric for Literature Circle Journals

Name _____ Date _____

0
- No journal

1
- Very little writing
- The work is sloppy
- There are no illustrations
- The writing does not relate to the book

2
- Includes at least two suggestions from the list
- Has incomplete drawings
- The ideas are not well-developed

3
- Includes at least four suggestions from the list
- Illustrations are complete and add meaning and interest
- The work is neat
- The ideas are well-developed
- Conventions are correct

Comments:

Figure 6.11 Rubric for Journal Responses

even top-notch. Have them evaluate it using the rubric in Figure 6.11. Then ask them to suggest criteria that are missing or revise the criteria to better reflect the work they're doing. Build your class rubric from what you and your students know and discover. For further examples of rubrics, we recommend *Classroom Based Assessment* (Hill, Ruptic, & Norwick, 1998).

Self-Reflection

Rubrics provide a concrete tool for self-reflection. We also need additional ways to help students develop the ability to look at their work with keen eyes. This is easier to do if we know how to do it with our own work. Being reflective means being willing to stop and look. "What am I looking for?" is a question many ask. Start with general prompts such as: "What one or two things do you like about your journal entry? Why?" Another useful prompt is: "What do you notice as you re-read your journal entry?" If you've already introduced rubrics, ask students to talk about their journal entry using some of the language of the rubric.

Build this ability to self-reflect naturally by talking about what you notice when looking at a journal entry. We encourage you to make a transparency of one of your own reading responses and talk about one or two things that seem effective to you ("I used a passage from the story to explain my ideas." "This week I tried a new prompt and wrote three sentences about it."). Then ask your students to point out anything they think "works."

Sharing your own work with your students requires you to take a deep, brave breath. Your students will love it, however. It sends a powerful message saying, "Journal entries are worth reading and doing . . . for the teacher too!"

There is also value in noticing something that didn't work or wasn't effective in your journal entry, then considering what to do about it ("Oh, now that I look at it again I notice it's not clear which character I'm talking about. I need to be sure to include the character's name."). Invite students to select one of their journal entries and look at it closely. Create a list (chart paper works well for this) of the things students notice. Remember to focus their talk on what's effective. Once this list is made, you may want to re-write it by categorizing the ideas students offer. Use student ideas, as well as ones you add, to begin the list of criteria for journal entries.

Some Final Thoughts on Response Journals

We know it takes time to teach students to write journal entries that result from active, interactive, reading. We're also aware it takes a commitment to ensure that journal entries are read and used to enrich literature circle discussions. When you introduce and demonstrate open-ended prompts, when you suggest new questions to ponder, and when you invite students to explore their interpretations through sketches and other diverse responses, you encourage your students to become thoughtful readers. This then becomes a significant goal—a goal that's feasible when we arm students with additional ways to discover what books mean and when we offer new tools to ignite discussions.

What is worth worrying about?

- Make sure responses serve a purpose and have an audience.
- Show and tell with actual examples.
- Beware of overkill—Less might be more.
- Realize that repeated experience and a focus on criteria provides the support for more meaningful responses.
- Understand how good books and good questions play a role in depth of response.
- Include variety in response formats. When responses seem dull or trivial or stale, take action!

What is worth letting go?

- The need to read and respond to everything students write in their journals.
- Responses that become full-blown projects, costly in terms of time, effort, and resources.
- The belief that quantity is the goal—more journal responses may not result in better responses.
- The notion you have to include every idea featured in this chapter in your literature circles classroom.

Common Questions About Response Journals

What should journals look like? Are spiral notebooks best? What if I don't have the money to buy a notebook or folder for each student?

There's no perfect journal. While spiral notebooks seem ideal, in some ways they can limit response, especially if sketches or responses other than writing are encouraged. We've all had students who simply can't draw if the paper has lines on it!

Many teachers we work with create a folder for each literature circle unit. Folders are constructed by including both lined and unlined paper on the inside and covering these pages with construction paper (see Chapter 3, Figure 3.16 for an example of a simply-constructed journal). This is easy to assemble by using staples or paper fasteners. (The benefit of paper fasteners is the ease with which you can add additional paper.) Students can then create their version of a new book jacket by drawing on the folder cover.

Paper folders with pockets also work well for journals and they can be purchased in bulk fairly inexpensively. Pockets allow students a ready place to keep their pencil, Post-its, and any other tools to guide journal entries (e.g., prompts, criteria sheets). Some teachers use pocket folders as the "container" for all literature circles materials—the book, discussion tools (bookmark, Post-it Notes), and journal entries.

My students don't seem to write meaningful responses. They hurry to get them done and then they're only one or maybe two sentences long. What can I do about that?

Kirstin Gerhold found this was the case with her fifth graders. As she tried to figure out why, she realized a few things. "By the time fifth grade rolls around, it's easy to assume kids have been writing about books for a long time. We can't take for granted they know how to do what we assign or what we mean when we ask them to write meaningful responses." The most logical way to combat this frustration is to teach what you mean by "meaningful" and to demonstrate strategies.

One possibility is to think about how journals are used during discussion. Consider having students use their journals entries to focus discussion, then suggest they add on to their journal response immediately following the discussion, while new ideas are still fresh in their mind. Another possibility is to demonstrate how to support one-sentence responses with specifics from the book or from their lives. Lori Scobie's lesson illustrating the difference between in-depth journal entries and quick notations in discussion logs is a good example of one way to do this (see pages 72–74).

My students are so sick of journals by the time they come to me. They've kept them in every grade and for every subject. How do I convince them (and myself) of their value and how do I help them to become interested, willing, maybe even eager to keep one again?

We've all felt the frustration of overkill. Since journals and response logs have become valued as thinking tools, it's likely our students will be asked to use them in all grades and for different subjects. If students don't see the purpose of keeping a journal and if they never have a use for them, then it's no wonder they balk when we assign such work. We suggest that you become thoughtful about the amount of writing and sketching you require. One good entry per week is a lot more valuable than 2 or 3 hurried entries. We also suggest you demonstrate how you use a response journal to deepen your understanding as a reader. And, of course, be sure your students use their journal responses in literature circle discussions as well as in whole class debriefings.

In addition, consider how variety creates new interest. By introducing sketching and other forms of response, you expand students' notions of what constitutes a journal entry. This, alone, may produce the results you desire: less whining and new thinking.

I notice you don't list summary work as one of your journal entry suggestions. Why not?

The biggest reason for this is because summary work isn't the goal of literature circles. We view literature discussion and response as critical, creative processes. We've also learned that summary entries do little to spark discussions, to prompt inquiry, to maintain readers' interest beyond the words on the page. Summarizing often requires students to rely on literal level comprehension, certainly important but limiting for active, insightful readers. Since we believe all children can—and do—respond beyond literal understanding, we structure journal entries in ways to encourage this.

What about published literature guides? Couldn't I use those questions and those assignments?

Published literature guides have become readily available for nearly every book we've used (and will eventually use) with literature circles. The temptation to rely on the teaching ideas and questions listed in these guides is great, maybe even greater given the energy you'll expend getting literature circles off the ground. Remember, readers play a critical role in the reading transaction. Just as important, authors who write literature guides have never met and don't know your students, their interests, needs, and questions. Your students are capable of raising questions about the books they're reading. They're also capable of engaging in lively discussions and creating unexpected responses. It's this sense of student choice, ownership, and discovery that we relish—and work to create.

How much time should I allow for journal responses?

Journal responses take time. The key is to make sure they're worth the time they take. This means you may need to re-think how you've structured time to teach and use journals. Start by requiring one journal response a week, and teach to that response. As you and your students become more adept with responses, and when they discover the value of such work to guide their discussions, you may want to increase the quantity you expect.

Should students write in their journals before they discuss or after or does it matter?

Believe it or not, it really doesn't matter. There are benefits and discoveries that result from both. When responses are written prior to discussion, they're more likely to be read or used to enhance the discussion. When they're written after the discussion, they often gain their shape from ideas raised during discussion. When this occurs, the discussion serves as a pre-write or a journal prompt. We suggest you try both and, when you debrief with your students, ask them what they notice and what they find works most effectively for them.

I don't have any examples of good journal entries to show my students. What can I do?

Once you involve your students with written and extended responses, you'll compile many useful examples. In the meantime, we recommend using the examples in this book and others. We also suggest using your own examples, realizing how powerful your example can be. You don't need to devote an evening's work in order to create the "perfect" response. There's great value in creating an impromptu response in front of your students, which will show them how you actually write.

Do I have to read and respond to every journal entry?

Somewhere in our teaching careers we've been led to believe that we must read each and every word our students write or we're not doing our job. The reality is: This isn't always possible nor is it always necessary. Of course, how much you read and respond depends upon the amount your students write and your purpose for reading and commenting on responses.

We consider the following as exceptions to this "don't read everything" suggestion. Since younger students usually write much less than older students, it's less time consuming to read and comment on their responses. For students who are new to journal responses, the value comes when comments guide, extend, and nudge their thinking. In addition, as students try out new response forms, your feedback helps them shape that type of response. In these situations we suggest making time to read and comment on every student's work. The benefits of reading all responses include providing an audience for students' work and discovering if they "get it," as well as whether your teaching had any effect.

When students write three or more responses during one literature circle unit, ask them to select the one response they'd like you to read. To do this they need to re-read and think about what they've written. Students can mark their passage with a paper clip or a Post-it. When you offer this option, introduce it during a focus lesson. Ask students to brainstorm what they might consider when making such a selection. Write out their ideas, then make the list available as they select. If you've introduced rubrics for journal entries, you can also suggest that students make their selection based on the criteria listed in the rubric.

How do I know what to write to students in response to their journal entries?

We once heard Donald Graves say, "What writers want are readers, not judges, of their work." This is just as true for our students. We recommend that you respond to journal entries as a "reader over their shoulder." Make it your purpose to acknowledge one of their ideas ("I remember when something like that happened to me too. It really hurts!") or to raise a question you don't have the answer to ("What is it about Caleb that reminds you of your brother?").

Just as we encourage readers to agree or disagree with each other during discussions, we believe your responses to journal entries can do that as well. The key is to nudge further thinking or clarification ("You call Palmer a wimp. I'm not sure I'd agree. How do *you* define a wimp and how does Palmer fit that definition?").

Response begets response. Whenever we respond to journal entries with interest and honesty—even if only briefly—we not only model other ways to think about the book, we keep response alive. Vicki Yousoofian believes her comments on journal entries hold her first graders more accountable as she expresses interest, praise, and confidence in their writing. Sixth grade teacher Janine King calls her comments a "feedback loop." She claims the benefits pay off when she responds personally and as a real audience.

CHAPTER 7

Focus Lessons: Incorporating Literacy Strategies

Teaching needed skills and strategies is not the same as fragmentation through drills and worksheets. Skills and strategies are taught in the literacy context . . . We don't always have to wait for a need to "come up" in the literature or writing. If we know students will need it, we can teach it through a focus lesson. Of course, it's a given that knowing what and when to teach depends on a highly knowledgeable and observant teacher.

—Regie Routman,
Literacy at the Crossroads (1996, p. 49)

As you've probably noticed by now, nearly every chapter of this book mentions the value of focus lessons as the way to teach literature circles components, and related strategies. In addition, most chapters also include an example or two of what such teaching looks like. We include these examples because we've experienced the benefits of focus lessons to establish and clarify instructional guidelines, demonstrate processes, and even support previous learning. This chapter examines how instruction in successful literature circles practices builds strategies for a range of literacy skills and applications.

What Are Focus Lessons? Why Do Them?

Defining a focus lesson is pretty easy, actually. A focus lesson targets instruction in one area and emphasizes strategies used in authentic situations. All of the focus lessons we feature reflect skills and strategies used by proficient readers and writers as they learn in literature circles. Notice that our emphasis is on teaching students to become proficient, strategic, active language users.

While the term may be somewhat new, focus lessons certainly aren't. Lucy Calkins (1986) coined the term "mini-lessons" to characterize the brief, focused nature of teaching young writers one skill or strategy at a time, then stepping away to allow students to use what was learned in an authentic writing situation. Such lessons direct students' attention to one specific aspect of what they're learning. Regie Routman (1996) speaks of such teaching opportunities as "focus lessons" and concentrates on the intentional nature of the teaching over its brevity. And years before these terms were created, apprentices learned their craft in a similar fashion. A mentor, or master teacher, noticed what they needed to become proficient, then set about teaching through demonstration.

We'd be surprised if you didn't learn a few things in your life in an apprenticeship model. For example, your bike riding mentors noticed that you were wearing out the toes of your shoes as you slowed your bike to a stop. "Time to learn how to brake," was their thought. So, they offered braking as the next lesson, perhaps first explaining the braking process, then climbing on the bike: "Watch what I do. . . . See? . . . Notice how I . . . Now, it's your turn."

In a similar fashion, we see focus lessons for literature circles consisting of the following components:

- Brief introduction

- Discussion, explanation, and/or demonstration of a strategy

- Opportunity to use the strategy

A focus lesson is best if it's kept short and specific. Most of us can only handle receiving so much information at a time while we're learning something new. The same is true for our students. If you limit your focus lesson so that it is from five to fifteen minutes long, you won't run out of time for students to use the ideas and information you've presented in the lesson. You also won't lose their attention nor will you overwhelm your students with too many concepts at once. Remember, you can (and probably will) return to a focus lesson in order to re-teach and build from as you offer another strategy or "tip" to guide students as they work toward independence.

Where Do Focus Lessons Come From?

If you consider how apprentices learn their craft, you'll notice that each lesson the "master" teaches is determined by what's needed. This means the teacher is observant and notices the needs of the apprentice, and then teaches to those needs. It seems simple enough, yet we're aware it can take years of practice to gain the ability to target teaching decisions based solely on what you observe and assess. It also takes trust. In an educational climate laden with teachers' manuals, published literature discussion guidelines, and documents featuring lists of student objectives, it's easy to think that the people who have written them know more about your students—or at least about teaching—than you do. The reality is, you have more access to, and knowledge about, your students than any publisher or author of these guides. We don't suggest you ignore such materials. Rather, we recommend that if you use them, do so as resources, selecting ideas in response to what your students need. In the meantime, we hope you'll trust your skills of observation and make teaching decisions based on those observations.

To aid your observation, and to offer another resource, we've categorized the types of focus lessons most commonly used by teachers for literature circles. Perhaps these lists will extend your notion of what's worthy of being taught.

Types of Focus Lessons

The array of possible focus lessons for literature circles is endless and dynamic. However, it's not very helpful to offer an exhaustive list, especially if you're still fairly new to all of this. So, we've compiled a few ideas gleaned from teachers who are getting started with literature circles. These lists may not include everything your students need. What they will offer are possibilities, examples of the range of topics addressed when you provide focus lessons related to literature circles.

The focus lesson categories we include in this chapter are:

- Literature Circle Procedures

- Reading, Writing, and Response Strategies

- Literature Qualities—Story Structure, Literary Elements, Memorable Language, Genre Characteristics

Literature Circle Procedures

At the first of the year, as well as during the first round or two of literature circles, it's important to teach students the procedures they need in order to get started. While it's easy to assume students know things such as how to move to their discussion area quickly and efficiently, it doesn't always happen. Rather than becoming frustrated, focus your energy on a brief lesson. State the problem, then request suggestions and strategies to resolve the issue. Such lessons make clear what you expect—and assume—and include students in the process. Other procedural focus lessons are noted in Figure 7.1.

Focus Lessons:
Literature Circle Procedures

- How to choose a book
- How to start discussion quickly
- How to listen attentively
- How to keep the conversation going
- The role of a discussion group member
- What to write in your response journal
- What to do when you don't understand
- What to do when your group finishes
- How to mediate conflicts
- How to spice up a lagging discussion
- How to tie extension projects back to the book

Figure 7.1 Focus Lessons on Literature Circle Procedures

It's important to establish procedures early, as it sets the standard for literature circles. Therefore, some of these lessons need to be taught at the beginning of the year and others will be scattered throughout the year as you see the need arise. Once these basic procedures are in place, teachers usually shift their focus to the skills, strategies, and qualities of active reading and response. Figure 7.2 presents a selection of possible focus lessons related to these aspects of literature circles.

Reading, Writing, and Response Strategies

While previous chapters include examples of focus lessons to guide students in oral and written response, there are many natural opportunities to introduce or review reading strategies during literature circles. The strategies listed in Figure 7.2 benefit students at all grade levels.

For example, Lori Scobie noticed many of her fourth graders making quick guesses about what they thought was going to happen next in their books. She knew that her

Focus Lessons: Reading Strategies	Focus Lessons: Writing and Response Strategies
• Predicting • Reading on to see if predictions make sense • Self-correcting when reading doesn't make sense • Thinking about what would make sense • Using what you already know (background knowledge) • Finding evidence to support a point • Comparing/contrasting • Identifying important information • Using flexible strategies to identify unknown words • Previewing • Building vocabulary through reading • Creating pictures in your head • Asking yourself (or the text) questions • Reading what you don't know slowly and what you do know quickly • Analyzing, interpreting, inferring	• Choosing a topic or focus for your journal entry • Supporting ideas with information from the book, your own life, or other books • Elaborating by using details • Writing with a purpose and for an audience • Trying out dialogue • Using figurative, descriptive language • Using sketches and illustrations to spark or extend ideas • Developing criteria for effective writing • Writing a response from a character's point of view • Incorporating ideas from Post-it Notes into a written response • Incorporating ideas raised during discussion into written response

Figure 7.2 Focus Lessons: Reading, Writing, and Response Strategies

students could become more strategic if they learned to support their predictions with more than a guess. She used a focus lesson to teach how this could be done.

Lori introduced her focus lesson directly: "Today we'll work on making predictions." She pointed to the class-created "Expert Reader Strategies" chart taped to a wall in the front of the classroom (see Figure 7.3). As she read the strategies aloud, she stopped after the second one, "Make predictions." Lori reminded her students that they'd talked about predictions earlier in the year but, based on some of the discussions she had heard, it was time to work on predictions again.

She asked, "How is a prediction different from a guess?" Her fourth graders took their time answering. Finally one student responded, "It's a *really smart* guess and you have to think for awhile." Lori extended this response by stating that valuable predictions are usually "really smart guesses" that are supported with evidence from the literature. "You see," Lori said, "that's the other side of predicting. You don't just take a guess and go on. You ask yourself, 'How did I know that?' and 'What does the author include to make me think my prediction is possible?'"

Lori then invited her students to try supporting their predictions with examples from a book they had never read. She pulled out a copy of *The Kid in the Red Jacket* (Park, 1987) and read the first page aloud. Students were asked to predict what might

Figure 7.3 Expert Reader Strategies Chart

happen next based on only the first page of the book. They had no trouble with this. So then Lori asked, "How will predictions help you as an expert reader?" Amanda stated, "It helps you understand the story more. You can see if you're right. You look at the story and it goes through your head more." Brad added, "If they give you clues, it gets you going faster at the end. You know that your prediction is right." Another student wrapped it up with, "If you predict, it helps you stick with the story."

Lori turned back to the chart (see Figure 7.3) and pointed out two other strategies, "Use context to figure out new words" and "Find evidence to support a point." Before she sent her students to their discussions, she mentioned that these two strategies were closely related to making predictions. "Expert readers use context and they find support—those are two things that make predictions useful." Students took this new (or renewed) knowledge and went back to work.

Literature Qualities—Story Structure, Literary Elements, Memorable Language, Genre Characteristics

Since literature circles provide an intensive opportunity to spend time with a book, it's natural to introduce your students to the qualities of literature. The teachers we work with have taught focus lessons on a range of topics related to literary qualities, from how stories are structured to what makes them memorable. The list we've prepared in Figure 7.4 includes four categories related to literature: story structure, literary elements, memorable language, and genre characteristics. As with our list of focus lessons on reading, writing, and responding strategies, these are only suggestions. Your own list will evolve based on what you discover your students need and are most interested in understanding about literature.

Focus Lessons: Literature Qualities
Story Structure, Literary Elements,
Memorable Language, Genre Characteristics

Story Structure
- Beginnings
- Climax
- Endings
- Problem/Attempts to solve problem
- Beginning, middle, end

Literary Elements
- Character, plot, setting, theme
- Point of view and perspective
- Tone and Mood
- Persuasive devices

Memorable Language
- Interesting words and phrases
- Action verbs
- Descriptive details
- Alliteration
- Simile/Metaphor/Analogy
- Synonyms

Genre Characteristics
- Realistic Fiction
- Historical Fiction
- Fantasy/Science Fiction
- Traditional Literature (myth, legend, tale)
- Poetry
- Biography/Autobiography
- Informational Books

Figure 7.4 Focus Lessons: Literature Qualities

Components of a Focus Lesson

Carol Avery, in her book *And With a Light Touch: Learning About Reading, Writing and Teaching with First Graders* (1993), identifies four qualities of effective mini (or focus) lessons: brevity, focus, gentleness of tone, and responsive selection.

Brevity.   When the concept of "mini-lessons" first appeared in professional literature, it was suggested that they last no more than five minutes. This limit may be more the hope than it is the reality. The key to a valuable focus lesson is to provide enough instruction and demonstration to give students ideas, information, and a strategy they can use. The teachers we work with aim to balance brevity with effectiveness. Length of time may depend on how much you include your students' ideas in the lesson and the extent of your demonstration. Lori Scobie's focus lesson on predictions took about ten minutes and then she sent the students off to their discussions.

Focus   Even though your students may need to learn more than it is possible for you to teach at one time, avoid the urge to teach too many strategies in one lesson. In her informative chapter on mini-lessons, Carol Avery contends that brevity and simplicity are important (1993, p. 118). She refers to a student teacher who once presented a mini-lesson on writing that lasted thirty-five minutes. When the lesson ended, the students were overwhelmed by the amount of information given. They were also left with only ten minutes to write.

A direct, clear, concise focus lesson is the goal, with enough time left over for students to use what was taught. Think of focus lessons as your opportunity to pass along useful reading, writing, and responding tips. The most helpful tips are short and they relate to something learners need and can use immediately. Lori's focus was specific to prediction. While it wasn't the first time her class had discussed predicting, it was the first time she focused on the difference between guesses and predictions. Just that one tidbit of information was enough to nudge students to read and predict, paying more attention to text.

Gentle in Tone.   If we believe that focus lessons are "invitations, not mandates" (Avery, 1993, p. 133), then we offer teaching tips with a tone that's informative, interesting, and worth the time and effort we're asking students to take. This becomes easier when your focus is geared to aspects of learning you've noticed are alive (or need to be brought to life) in your classroom. It's harder to keep the tone invitational when focus lessons come from what's listed next in the teacher's manual rather than from what your students are doing. Notice how easily Lori introduced the concepts behind making supported predictions. Her lesson grew out of what she noticed during her literature circle discussions. It was presented by including her students' ideas, building upon what they said, and using their language—"smart guesses"—to extend their notions of predicting. Then she provided a quick chance to try out the new information. Lori's tone said, "I know you already know some of this. Let's review and add onto what we know and then try it out." The invitation to learn was extended and her students took it.

Responsive Selection.   Effective focus lessons grow out of the needs of the students in your class. Lori's idea to offer a focus lesson on "smart guess" predicting, using evidence from the book, grew out of listening in on discussions and reading journal responses. Such teaching always keeps learners and learning in the forefront. This necessitates careful observation and some note taking to discover whether there is a lone student in need of assistance, or a group of students (maybe the entire class) who are ready for some guided instruction. Focus lessons represent responsive teaching that directs instruction to the need.

Keeping Track of Focus Lessons

There is value in devising some means of keeping track of the focus lessons you teach as well as when you teach—and re-teach—them. If anything, it provides you with a sense of student needs and how and when you address them. We all know how many things teachers try to remember, including whether or not they've taught something they knew needed to be taught.

You do not need an elaborate form or system to keep track of the focus lessons you present. You can simply make a running list of each lesson's focus inside the front cover of your lesson planning book. Or, if you're interested in categorizing focus lessons, you could photocopy Figures 7.1, 7.2, and 7.4 and write the date you taught a lesson immediately next to the area of focus. Since we know there's often a need to re-teach a focus lesson, we've devised a form that allows space for multiple dates (see Figure 7.5). We created this form by listing the focus lessons related to literature circles procedures, then allowing for three dates when we might teach (and re-teach) the lessons. A similar form can be made for focus lessons related to reading, writing, and responding strategies and for literature qualities.

Focus Lesson	Date	Date	Date
How to choose a book			
How to start discussion quickly			
How to listen attentively			
How to keep conversation going			
Role of group member			
What to write in response journal			
What to do when you don't understand			
What to do when your group finishes			
How to mediate conflicts			
How to spice up lagging discussions			
How to tie extension projects back to the book			

Figure 7.5 Focus Lessons Checklist

Some Final Thoughts on Focus Lessons

The most useful focus lessons evolve in response to students' needs and grow out of your daily observations of literature circles. There is value in taking the time to show and tell as you teach. When you do this in front of your students, you begin to demystify the practice of reading, writing, and responding. Don't be discouraged if you don't see an immediate application of what you attempted to teach in a focus lesson. Trust students to implement what they've learned over time, with experience, and as they see the need. And trust yourself to craft the type of lessons that will guide them as they learn.

What is worth worrying about?

- Make focus lessons intentional and explicit through demonstrations.
- Provide opportunity for students to practice what they learn immediately.
- Watch for focus lesson needs as you observe discussions and read journal entries.

What is worth letting go?

- The temptation to teach everything that readers and writers need through literature circle focus lessons.
- The notion that focus lessons must fit into a specific time frame. Work toward lessons that run between five and fifteen minutes and realize the dynamic nature of learning and teaching may result in lessons that run longer.
- The desire to teach more than learners can handle—and use—at one sitting.

Common Questions About Focus Lessons

My students don't know all the words in the books used for literature circles. How can I teach vocabulary during this time?

Since books selected for literature circles usually aren't those written with a controlled vocabulary scheme, you may discover your students won't know every word in the books they select. One benefit of literature circles is how discussions and response journals focus on meaning, not on reading word for word. This reminds readers that not knowing a word isn't cause for giving up. Teach students to become strategic when they're slowed down by an unknown word. They can use Post-its or bookmarks to list their "wonder words" (see Chapter 5 for information about using bookmarks and discussion logs to list such words). Then they bring these words to their literature circle discussion for help. You can also teach focus lessons on strategies to identify unknown words (e.g., using context clues, substituting the word with one you know, using letters and sounds to predict). Such lessons can be taught within the context of a literature circle discussion or offered for the entire class. You'll make this decision based on what you notice your students need.

I'm still not sure my students are comprehending what they read. How will I know if I don't use comprehension questions?

The underlying purpose of literature circles is reading for meaning. This occurs when readers talk, write, re-read, and extend understanding through extension projects. Since you won't be responsible for comprehension questions, you'll have to look elsewhere for evidence that your students understand what they read. The teachers we work with pay careful attention to the types of questions students raise during discussion. What students ask provides insight into the meaning they're making. How they answer each other's questions provides evidence too. Another place to glean information about students' comprehension is in their journal entries and extension projects. When open-ended prompts and guiding questions are used for discussions and journals, be sure that students include support for their response. You may need to teach some focus lessons on how to do this (e.g., cite evidence from the book, make a connection to another book, an event, something that's happened to you).

CHAPTER 8

Extension Projects

*. . . they are not hurried away from the lived-through aesthetic experi-
ence by being asked only to summarize and paraphrase. Rather, students are encouraged to reflect, listen, savor, explore, and contemplate,
then to respond to the work with new perspectives and understandings . . .*

—Amy A. McClure & Connie S. Zitlow,
Language Arts, 68 (1991, p. 28)

The value of literature circles is the opportunity they offer readers to extend and develop interpretation. Ending a literature circle unit with an extension project provides
readers additional ways to revisit what they've read, continue the conversations (and
the discoveries), and create even more meaning. In fact, we've observed some unique
and provocative interpretations when students use visual and performing arts as they
express their understandings and discoveries about what they've read.

This chapter will explore what can occur when readers extend their responses
after reading. It will also offer a selection of extension project possibilities, examine how
teachers guide students through the process of creating such aesthetic responses, and
suggest ways to assess and evaluate this aspect of literature circles.

Definitions and Benefits

One of the most frequently asked questions related to extension projects is, "How do
they differ from book reports?" What we know about book reports (and extension projects,
too, for that matter) is that they vary in purpose, type, and quality from classroom to
classroom. Even knowing this, there is value in clarifying what we've come to understand about both as activities to culminate the reading of a book. The chart in Figure 8.1
explains what we see as the similarities and differences between book reports and extension projects.

Teachers often assign book reports to assess whether students have read their
books. The audience is primarily the teacher. We understand there are many variants
to book reports and we don't propose that they be abandoned in classrooms. What we do
propose is a re-thinking of the purposes and audience for such projects, especially as
they relate to literature circles.

Extension projects are most valuable when they continue readers' responses, often
involving readers in the process of creating their response through the arts. Many teachers encourage (even require) students to create extension projects in collaboration with
the members of their literature circle team. For example, when Kirstin Gerhold's fifth
graders created a whole-class story quilt in response to their literature circle theme of
"Facing Hard Times with Courage," each group designed a border reflective of their
specific book. Through this collaboration, students continued their conversations about

Book Reports . . .	Literature Extension Projects . . .
Offer readers a chance to pause and reflect once initial reading is over	Offer readers a chance to pause and reflect once initial reading is over
Serve to prove that a book has been read	Serve to extend and deepen interpretation
Develop from a book read alone	Develop from a book read and discussed with others
Are crafted independently	Can be crafted independently or in collaboration with others
Rarely involve draft work, planning or rereading prior to project completion	Often require drafting of ideas and rereading prior to project completion
Have a limited audience: the teacher	Have an extended audience: other students, parents, teachers
Can be done without reading the book	Require reading, rereading, and even discussing with others to complete project

Figure 8.1 Comparing Book Reports and Extension Projects

the book as they planned and constructed aspects of the project together. We'll explore this process more in depth later in this chapter.

Following extension project completion, students share their work through presentations in which they inform each other about the books they've read and discussed. It's not uncommon for students in the audience to discover a book they want to read from seeing their classmates' projects and hearing the presentations. The extension projects (and the processes involved) also provide teachers with assessment information, which we'll also discuss later in this chapter.

Extension Project Possibilities

While many lists of extension projects are available, the length of these lists can feel staggering. We recognize the benefit of choice, but we also know how daunting too many choices can be. What we offer here is a selective list of extension projects recommended by teachers just getting started with literature circles. You'll notice that we don't specify a grade level for any of the projects. Experience has shown us that all of these projects work well for readers of varying ages. If you're interested in additional project possibilities and in diverse ways of deepening response through the arts, we recommend reading Chapters 10 and 11 in *Literature Circles and Response* (Hill et al., 1995).

We've divided the list of extension projects into two categories: projects that are most manageable for getting started (see Figure 8.2), and projects that are more complex (see Figure 8.3). Following these lists, we suggest some considerations for teaching the process and then provide examples of how different teachers structured two of these projects, one from the Getting Started list, the other from the More Complex list. You'll see how these teachers *teach* the processes so that their students come to know the planning, thinking, and creating involved in such work. This intentional teaching prepares students to create similar projects independently later on.

Getting Started Extension Projects

The first extension projects you present can be done individually or collaboratively since they aren't too complex nor do they require ongoing literary discussions. Some of the projects listed below can be completed within one or two class sessions; others deserve more time.

Getting Started Extension Projects

Accordion Book—Choose five to seven significant scenes from your book. Make an illustrated accordion-shaped book that reveals the sequence of your book's storyline. Include some written descriptions, such as: What's happening in the scene? Why is this scene important to you?

Bookmark—Create a bookmark featuring either your favorite character or the character you consider to be most significant in your book. Be sure to include the book title and author as well as the character's name and "portrait" or illustration. Adaptation: On the back of the bookmark, explain why you selected your featured character. (See Figures 8.6, 8.7, 8.9, and 8.10 for examples.)

Story Hat—Make a "newspaper hat" out of a piece of white butcher paper. At the top of the hat's front side, write the name of your book and the author. Divide the front brim into three sections. In the first section draw something that happened at the beginning of the book. In the middle section, draw something that happened in the book's middle. In the last section, draw the problem of the story. Then divide the brim on the back of your hat into two sections. In the first section, draw how the problem was solved. In the last section, draw something that happened in the end of your book. (See Figure 3.13 for an example.)

Figure 8.2 Getting Started Extension Projects

More Complex Extension Projects

Other projects (see Figure 8.3) work more effectively as whole class projects since they include more components, they require more time to complete, and they often involve returning to literature circle groups to discuss how information from the book can be represented. Because of their many components, the success of these more complex projects increases with careful, deliberate teaching and the allocation of enough time to do them justice. These projects may take up to a week to complete.

Extension Project Focus

We want students to understand that creating an extension project includes reflection, interpretation, and maybe even some rereading. In order to facilitate such thinking, we recommend that you take the time to teach these processes. Consider how third grade teacher, Adam Brauch, guided his students in thinking about the purpose of, and audience for, their extension projects. Rather than assume that his students know how to plan, he designed key questions to guide them. These questions included:

- How does my project show what I have learned from my book?
- In what ways does my project include information from my book?

More Complex Extension Projects

ABC Book—Create an alphabet book that focuses on key events, characters, ideas, and information from your book. Include an illustration on each page as well as one to two sentences explaining each letter of the alphabet.

CD Cover—Design the front and the back cover for a CD to capture the theme or spirit of your book. Be sure the name of the book, plus the title of the hit single, appears on the front cover along with an appealing sketch or design. On the back, list the other songs from the CD, making sure they relate to the book and to the characters' experiences. [Adaptation: Write lyrics to the hit single.]

Commemorative Stamp—Select a key character or scene, or focus on an important theme from your book, and develop a stamp to commemorate that character, scene, or theme. Include a picture, a selected phrase, and the stamp's value.

Jackdaw—Collect artifacts representing ideas, events, characters, and/or themes in your book. Prepare a display of these items. Label each artifact and briefly write about its importance to the book. You may also want to include a quote from your book for each of the artifacts.

Story Quilt—Create a quilt square featuring a chapter or significant scene from your book. Include a border with a repeated design or symbol that represents a key idea from your chapter or scene. Select an important quote (or write a brief summary) from your chapter and write it inside your quilt square. [Adaptation: Design a character quilt featuring both protagonists and antagonists, and major and minor characters from your book.] (See Figures 8.12 and 8.14 for examples.)

Figure 8.3 More Complex Extension Projects

- When someone views my project, what will they learn about my book?

Adam presented these three questions during a focus lesson early in the students' planning, and then he returned to the questions as he invited students to evaluate their work. In this way, he clarified his expectations and helped his students plan effective projects.

The Process of Extension Projects

We recognize there is a lot to consider as you create the structure for all of the components of literature circles. It's helpful to remember that while the planning seems time-consuming at first, over time you and your students will internalize the processes and discover your own ways of adapting them to best fit your needs. As you move in that direction, we invite you to try out the process ideas and questions listed in Figure 8.4. These are recommended by teachers who are fairly new to literature circles. We also include them because they're manageable and provide a structure that supports not just extension projects, but all aspects of literature circles.

First Steps

When you *first* begin to craft a structure for extension projects, the *most important* elements to consider are those listed in Figure 8.4.

Extension Project Process—First Steps

Setting Purpose
Ask: What do I want my students to focus on? What specific literary elements am I interested in teaching? What re-reading will they need to do?

Planning for Teaching
Ask: How can I guide students through the process? What steps are most valuable to complete this project? What materials will students need? How can I demonstrate the process? Do I need to create a sample or do I have a similar project I can show?

Setting a Time Frame
Ask: How much time do I need to explain and demonstrate? How much time do students need to complete each component of the project: drafting, discussing, creating, revising, producing?

Figure 8.4 First Steps

Almost all of the teachers we've worked with started slowly with this process.

Next Steps

When you're ready to add additional components to your planning process, you might find it valuable to consider the steps listed in Figure 8.5.

Extension Project Process—Next Steps

In addition to Setting Purpose, Planning for Teaching, and Setting a Time Frame, add:

Presenting the Projects
Ask: What audiences might be interested in seeing and hearing about the extension projects? How can I help students plan these presentations? What information do they need to include in their presentations? How do I keep presentations lively, fun, and celebratory?

Assessing and Evaluating the Projects
Ask: What do I value about the extension projects? What criteria should we use in our evaluations? How do I involve students in setting the criteria? How do I develop a form or checklist that identifies what should be evaluated? How do I include students in self-reflection? How can I involve students in providing evaluative feedback to each other?

Figure 8.5 Next Steps

Guiding Students Through the Process

The first time you involve your students with extension projects, select one project and literally walk students through the process of planning and creating. To show how some teachers have done this, we'll explain the process for two specific extension projects—bookmarks (a Getting Started Project) and story quilts (a More Complex Project)—both easily adapted for primary and intermediate students. Bookmarks are an ideal getting-started project to focus on character, setting, or personal response. Story quilts are a more complex project since they involve more components, take more time, and require more planning, rereading, and discussing.

Bookmarks—Focus on Character (with young readers)

Vicki Yousoofian introduced the character bookmark to culminate her first graders' third round of literature circles. Earlier in the year Vicki's students created a mobile and a story hat, both projects that focus on elements of literature. When Vicki planned the character bookmark project, she considered three key elements: purpose, teaching process, and time frame.

Purpose   Vicki selected the bookmark as a way to involve her students in specific thinking about character. This project was one that students created individually. Whether students who read the same book selected the same character or not didn't matter.

Teaching Process   Vicki introduced this project in a focus lesson during which she explained what she expected students to include: name, story title, character, reason for choosing character, illustration. As she talked about each element, Vicki showed her students a bookmark she'd created in response to a novel read in her adult book club. Then the students brainstormed ideas for their own bookmarks. After they shared their ideas, Vicki sent them off to work on their own, reminding them to go back to their books for additional ideas.

Time Frame   The entire process—introducing the project, guiding a discussion of ideas for each required element, and providing time for students to create their bookmark—took one class session of about forty minutes.

Figure 8.6
Bookmark of
Miss Hart *Ruby
the Copycat*
(Rathmann,
1991)

Figure 8.7
Bookmark of
Gloria *Officer
Buckle and
Gloria*
(Rathmann,
1995)

Bookmarks—Focus on Character (with older readers)

Janine King also chose character bookmarks as one of the first extension projects she tried with her sixth graders. This project was done early in the school year following a literature circle reading of *Roll of Thunder, Hear My Cry* (Taylor, 1976). In her planning, Janine took into account the following:

Purpose   Like Vicki, Janine also wanted her students to focus on character. The bookmark seemed like a project that wasn't too time-consuming but would still allow for some careful rereading and thinking specific to the book's characters, then narrowing to one character for focus.

Teaching Process   Prior to introducing the bookmark, Janine helped her students gather information about the book's significant characters. First, she asked her students to select four key characters, then use their response journals to gather information about each character (collecting quotes, listing adjectives, including examples of events the characters were involved in). Next, she asked students to choose two of the characters and compare and contrast them using a Venn diagram. Once these two processes were completed, she introduced the bookmark project.

Notice (Figure 8.8) how Janine's character bookmark components are similar to the ones Vicki used. Her teaching process was also similar. She introduced the required elements in a focus lesson and allowed time for her students to discuss each component by brainstorming ideas they might choose using characters from the current class read aloud *The Watsons Go to Birmingham—1963* (Curtis, 1995). Janine then showed her students a sample bookmark she'd made, featuring the character of Byron from the read-aloud book. Before reading the back of her bookmark, she asked her students to consider what they would have written had they selected Byron. She concluded the focus lesson by encouraging her students to sketch illustration ideas and write drafts of the character's description before creating their final bookmark. She also suggested that they do some rereading in their book and return to the ideas listed in their response journals and Venn diagrams to find information to include in their bookmarks.

Character Bookmark

Front
1) Write the name of an important character.
2) Draw that character.

Back
1) Explain why this character is important.
2) Tell your feelings about this character.
3) Describe the character.

Figure 8.8 Character Bookmark (older readers)

Time Frame   Janine set aside time during five class periods (approximately 45 minutes each) for students to complete the entire process—from drafting ideas to preparing a final copy of their bookmarks. While they worked, they also held culminating literature circle discussions. An example of a completed bookmark (front and back) from *Roll of Thunder, Hear My Cry* is shown in Figures 8.9 and 8.10.

Story Quilt (with young readers)

One of Vicki Yousoofian's final extension projects of the year was the story quilt. This project, along with the others done in Vicki's class, was selected by the teacher. It may first appear that Vicki doesn't allow for much student choice in these projects. However, she knows that she needs to guide students through the process of each project while

Big Ma is important
because she
helps people when
they're sick
and cares for
them when no
one else can.
She is the one
who keeps all
the blacks from
getting voilent. I
think that she
is a great character
in this book. She
heals, cares, understands
the sick. Her most
important feature
is her ability to
calm. She is a
big hearted
character that
can do nothing
but good.

| Figure 8.9 | Figure 8.10 |
| Character Bookmark (front) | Character Bookmark (back) |

offering choices about what book, what character, what scene, and what symbols they'll use. There is choice even within an assigned project.

Purpose   The story quilt project was selected to culminate a unit on fairy tales, folk tales, myths, and legends. Vicki's first graders had read a wide range of stories, including traditional tales, cultural variants, and modern/twisted versions. They'd created Venn diagrams to compare and contrast some of the tales and they'd read, illustrated, and written about others. Vicki then introduced a class story quilt, inviting each student to create a quilt square representing their favorite tale.

Process   As with the bookmark, Vicki introduced this extension project in a focus lesson by showing a chart of the required components (see Figure 8.11), then demonstrating how she approached each element.

Vicki began the class discussion by showing a quilt square she made from one of her students' favorite tales, *Jim and the Beanstalk* (Briggs, 1970). She asked questions such as, "Why is this a good symbol for the border?", "What other symbols could I have used?", "What else might I have drawn in the middle of my square?", "What are some possible lessons that Jim, the Giant, or even the mother learned in this story?" Then Vicki asked her students to select the tale they wanted to feature in their own quilt

---

Story Quilt

1. Pick a favorite fairy tale.

2. Make a border around your square (do this in pencil).

3. Pick one thing that is a *symbol* of the story. Use this *symbol* to make your border.

4. In the middle of your square, draw a picture of something in the story.

5. Write: The lesson in the story was _____.

6. On the back write your name and title of the fairy tale you chose.

Figure 8.11 Story Quilt Assignement (younger readers)

square. Prior to their written and sketched work, she involved students in some oral drafting of ideas, brainstorming what they might include for each component in their selected book. For example when she asked what symbols they might use, answers included, "a beanstalk" and "false teeth" (for *Jim and the Beanstalk,* [Briggs, 1970]), "a glass slipper" (for *Cinderella* [Ehrlich, 1985]), "a basket" and "a cloak" (for *Little Red Riding Hood* [McPhail, 1995]), and "a loafer" (for *Cinder Edna* [Jackson, 1994]). Figure 8.12 shows one of the first graders' quilt squares.

Figure 8.12
First Grader's
Story Quilt Square

Time Frame   The time allotted to introduce, discuss, and complete this class story quilt took three class periods of approximately 40 minutes each.

Story Quilt (with older readers)

Kirstin Gerhold also selected the story quilt project for her fifth graders. This project was the third extension project of the year and it concluded the reading of novels set during the Revolutionary War, focusing on the theme, "Facing Hard Times with Courage." Kirstin guided her students through each step of the process, working at a pace that allowed numerous opportunities to return to the book and to discussion groups for idea generating, revising, and focused thinking.

Purpose   Kirstin wanted her students to create a visual and written representation of their theme as depicted by the books they read. She introduced how symbols, colors, design choices, and language could all reflect "Facing Hard Times with Courage."

Process   Prior to introducing the quilt square project, Kirstin developed a planning sheet, listing the required components and recommended process (see Figure 8.13). She introduced each step during a focus lesson and allotted time for literature circle teams to meet and talk about ideas specific to their book. While Kirstin hadn't created a completed quilt square to show her students what a finished product might look like, she did draw a sample draft of the square, to demonstrate the idea of including a border, an illustration, and brief, yet focused writing. She had an idea where each component should be placed on the square and her sample draft demonstrated that to her students.

STORY QUILT RESPONSE PROJECT
"Facing Hard Times with Courage"

Assignment: You will be responsible for creating a quilt square about your book for a class-constructed paper story quilt. Each of you will choose a way to reflect the theme and create a square of a story quilt to illustrate the theme.

1. Meet with your group and discuss how the theme is represented in your book.

2. With your group, select a color for your quilt square border. As discussed in class, the color should represent some aspect of the theme. Select the symbols, designs, or illustrations from your book to include in your border.

3. Reread parts of your book or your journal to help you design the center of your quilt square. This design represents how the theme is brought to life. Pay attention to ideas, words, scenes, and images that seem especially significant.

4. Create a rough draft, including a visual and written response to the book: Visually, include a border and an illustration to portray your book and the theme. The written response will include a description of the illustration and how it represents the theme. The description of the illustration may be a quote or section from the book (with page number).

5. Using white paper distributed in class, create a colorful quilt square to commemorate your book and the theme.

Figure 8.13 Story Quilt Assignment

Time Frame   The entire process—from introducing the planning sheet to hanging the story quilt—took a week and a half of sessions lasting approximately 45 minutes per day.

Figure 8.14 shows a student's quilt square.

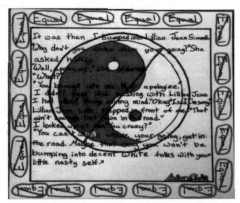

Figure 8.14
Story Quilt Square

Extension Project Presentations

Just as we want to talk to someone when we read a good book, we also like to share work we've done that matters to us. When students invest time and effort in projects that they feel proud to share, they deserve opportunities to do just that, with audiences that may include their classmates, students in other classes, parents, and (of course) their teacher. Guiding students to understand the focus of a project and then supporting them in the steps that the project entails, eventually leads to projects presented with vitality and confidence. We encourage you to consider presentations as literary celebrations with a dual purpose for the literature circle members: to showcase their book and to invite audience members to regard the book as one they might want to read, too.

One way to clarify presentation components is to introduce them in a focus lesson. The first time Lori Scobie's fourth graders presented their projects, she asked them to consider what would be important to make their presentations effective. They came up with the following list: Has information about the book, speak loudly with eye contact, presentation is polished, visuals need to be colorful.

Once they drafted this list, Lori and her students discussed what each element meant and came up with examples of what they'd expect as quality work. Interestingly, this list wasn't brand new. Instead, it grew out of the criteria Lori's students had developed earlier in the year for presentations in other content areas work. In fact, the first item is the only "new" item to the list, but it was one the fourth graders included because it was specific and essential to literature circles.

Lisa Norwick (1996) has explored literature circles when teaching both primary and intermediate grades. She offers the following structure for her students' extension project celebrations. Perhaps you'll find some ideas from her structure to serve your purposes.

Celebration of Extension Projects

- Tell listeners/viewers the title and author of your book.
- Introduce the members of your extension project team.
- Offer a *brief* summary of your book.
- Share your project.
- Invite comments and questions from your audience.

There's no one best set of guidelines to use in structuring project presentations. We recommend that you take a look at the examples given here and ask your students to offer their ideas. Don't be surprised if your class suggests some of the ideas included in these examples—in fact, they may even have better ones. The key is to keep the guidelines simple and clear, discuss the components, use specific examples, and demonstrate what you expect. The other important point is to keep the presentations lively, fun, and celebratory. After all, this is the time for students to show off their books and their work!

Assessing and Evaluating Extension Projects

Involvement in extension projects and presentations provides numerous opportunities for assessment and evaluation. Planning and creating the extensions provides information about comprehension, interpretation, and even active reading. One way to gather this information is to roam the room during project work time, listening in on conversations, and taking anecdotal notes. However, many of the teachers represented in this book have set anecdotal note taking as their goal for *next* year, selecting instead to invest their time and energy this first year on organizing and managing all of the components of literature circles.

There are some uncomplicated ways to gather assessment and evaluation data from extension projects. These range from asking students some basic self-reflection questions to developing criteria checklists.

Self-Reflection

One of the most useful getting-started self-reflections we've seen was developed by Lisa Norwick (1996) when she taught sixth graders. She also used these same questions when she taught second grade. As Lisa has learned, clear, thought-provoking questions aren't specific to a reader's age or grade level. Lisa's self-reflections include just two questions:

1. What is something you're proud of from your project?
2. What is something you learned from someone else's project that you might want to try next time?

Like it or not, students can exert great energy apologizing for what didn't go well, rather than focusing on their positive efforts. Lisa's first question invites students to identify an area of strength or a specific quality of their work. Students' answers may give you information you may not have selected for focus. For example, what we notice as interesting or well-crafted may not be what matters to our students. Sometimes their selections include criteria we hadn't considered using, such as when they point out an area that's "good" because it's what they worked on the hardest. Lisa's second question indirectly asks students to pay careful attention to others' presentations. In essence, this gives them a purpose for listening while it also summons them to consider what else is possible.

Kirstin Gerhold created an extension project debriefing form that serves a similar purpose for her fifth graders (see Figure 8.15). Notice how the questions adapt ideas from Lisa's questions, yet also seek more information.

Extension Project Self-Reflection

1. Did your project turn out the way you hoped it would?
2. What is something about your project that you are proud of?
3. How was your experience working in a group (or alone)?
4. What size group would you like to work in on the next project? Why?
5. What is a goal for your next literature extension project?

Figure 8.15 Self-Reflection Questions

These are by no means the best, nor the only, questions you could ask. In designing a self-reflection form for your students, we recommend the following:
- Consider what questions best reflect your students' projects.
- Limit the form to only a few questions.
- Introduce the questions in a focus lesson.
- Provide adequate time for students to think through their responses.

Criteria Checklists

Kirstin Gerhold teaches in a school where she's expected to assign grades on extension projects as well as in report cards. Given this, she develops criteria checklists with point values to clarify her expectations as well as demonstrate the relative weight of each criterion. Just as you invite your students to develop guidelines for discussions and project presentations, a form can be designed in concert with your students. When you include student input, they become clearer about expectations and they develop a growing understanding of what evaluation entails.

Kirstin created a form specifically for the story quilt project and it includes evaluative response from both teacher and student (see Figure 8.16).

Evaluation of Presentations

Just as we encourage students to have a voice in their own evaluation, much can be learned when we invite students to provide evaluative feedback to others. Lori Scobie created an evaluation checklist that reflects the guidelines she and her students constructed (see Figure 8.17). Because the statements are very general, this checklist can easily be used for each literature circle unit, or it can be adapted by adding criteria specific to each project.

Some Final Thoughts on Extension Projects

Opportunities to create an extension project in response to the reading of a book can interest your students in ways that talking and writing cannot. Whether the project is one they can complete in one or five class sessions, whether they work alone or collaborate with their literature circle team members, whether they're nervous about sharing their work in front of an invited audience or calm as can be . . . these aren't the important things. What is important is the opportunity you offer when you ask your students

Name _____

Literature Circle Story Quilt
"Facing Hard Times with Courage"

Self-Evaluation	Teacher Evaluation

• Illustrations _____ (20)
• Includes border and main illustration
 	
• Illustrations relate to theme
• Border includes symbols and colors
 	
  that the group chose
	Illustrations _____ (20)
	• Includes border and main illustration
	• Illustrations relate to theme
	• Border includes symbols and colors
	
	  that the group chose

Written Description _____ (20)
• Quality of writing
  Includes explanation of illustration
• Grammar
  spelling, punctuation, sentence structure
	Written Description _____ (20)
	• Quality of writing
	  Includes explanation of illustration
	• Grammar
	  spelling, punctuation, sentence structure

Time and Effort _____ (5) • Neatness • Details	Time and Effort _____ (5) • Neatness • Details
Creativity _____ (5)	Creativity _____ (5)
Total points _____ (50)	Total points _____ (50) Overall percentage

On the Back: In what ways does your quilt square represent the theme, "Facing Hard Times with Courage"?

Figure 8.16 Student and Teacher Evaluation Form

Book Celebration Presentation Evaluation

The presenter: _____

1. Spoke loudly and clearly	1 2 3 4 5
2. Has good eye contact	1 2 3 4 5
3. Showed the visual aid well	1 2 3 4 5
4. Looked practiced and organized	1 2 3 4 5
5. Had all the information and it made sense	1 2 3 4 5

Average score: _____

The best thing this presenter did was: _____

_____

Figure 8.17 Book Presentation Evaluation

to pause at the end of their reading and create something that brings their book to life, not only for themselves, but also for those who are lucky enough to hear, view, and read the extension project. It is in this way that you culminate—as well as celebrate—literature and literature circles.

What is worth worrying about?

- Set a clear purpose for projects and remember they serve to *extend* what's been read.
- Guide students to see extension projects as more than fun art activities.
- Think through the process necessary to create a significant project, even for the projects that seem less complex.
- Find ways for students who may not shine through traditional processes (writing, talking) to demonstrate what they know and comprehend (through art, drama, dance).
- Remember the importance of time—time to teach, time to discuss ideas, time to create, time to present.

What is worth letting go?

- Realize that extension projects do not have to be elaborate to fulfill their purpose.
- Worrying about your own artistic ability can get in the way of introducing projects your students can do. It also denies you the opportunity to show how everyone can interpret creatively, without placing the focus on talent or ability.
- Waiting until you create or find a perfect model to show as an example can result in your students never being introduced to new ideas.
- Total student choice may result in missed opportunities to teach a process and to provide a specific focus.

Common Questions About Extension Projects

How can I organize the time so all literature circle groups finish at the same time?
One way to work toward projects being completed on the same day is to set a target deadline with your students, monitor their progress, and adjust the deadline as more or less time is needed. For example, many teachers let students know that they have five class sessions to work, then they help their students consider how best to divide the project components into manageable tasks.

I don't have much money for extension project materials. Can I still do extensions?
The extension projects we've featured in this chapter are not costly nor do they require specialized materials. Even fairly extensive projects, such as the story quilt, require the type of paper that most schools keep in stock—plain white paper, construction paper, and perhaps butcher paper for a background.

How can I encourage students to reread when they're doing extension projects?
This can be done both through the planning sheets as well as during the oral discussions and explanations of the project's process. Ask questions that include an expectation of evidence: "What pages in your book do you need to reread?" "Where in your book can you find ideas to use in this project?" "What specific information do you remember from your book that will help you with this project?"

Do students work on projects at home?

Most teachers we've worked with encourage all work to be done at school. One reason for this is to "control" the project so that the students themselves (and not well-meaning parents) do the work. The focus here is on your students' interpretation and exploration, rather than on producing the "prettiest" or most elaborate project. Also, whenever you provide time for project work at school, you encourage continued discussion about the book.

How can I foster quality artistic responses?

If you're just getting started with literature circles, this might not be your most important focus. However, if you are intrigued about developing your students' sense of artistic quality in their responses, we recommend choosing one element to focus upon, perhaps color choice or selecting the medium that best reflects ideas or themes in the book. For some additional ways to deepen and extend artistic response, turn to Chapters 10 and 11 in *Literature Circles and Response* (Hill et al., 1995).

What if the student does a quality artistic presentation but doesn't hit the substance of the book? Or, what if they choose a project that doesn't "fit" their book?

Students' growing understanding of the purpose for extension projects means they may make some choices that are less-than-substantive during their early attempts. With careful planning and the overseeing of these plans, with frequent reminders of purpose, by showing other examples, and with numerous experiences, we assist students in developing projects that become more substantial and fitting.

How do you guarantee that students take these projects seriously?

While there is no sure guarantee, we've found that when students have choices there is a greater chance they'll invest time and energy. Other factors include asking for and using students' ideas when establishing the criteria for evaluation and providing adequate time to create substantial projects. Our students are often no different than we are; when things matter to us and when we invest our time and energy into them, we take them seriously.

Final Thoughts . . .

You only need a few resources to help you take those first steps in literature circles:

- Your belief in the value of reading, talking about, and responding to good books with a community of learners;
- Your belief in your students; and
- Your belief in yourself.

With those in place, the rest will follow. We hope that the teachers whose voices you've heard in this book have given you many new ideas—and reinforced old ones.

When the answers you discover prompt even more questions, you'll probably want additional resources. Seek out colleagues who will explore literature circles with you. Ask everyone you know what professional resources they have sitting on their shelves, so marked up with Post-it notes and highlights that you can barely see the pages. Here are the books we turn to ourselves and recommend to teachers:

. . . on literature circles:

Daniels, Harvey. (1994). *Literature circles: Voice and choice in the student-centered classroom*. York, ME: Stenhouse.

Hill, Bonnie Campbell, Johnson, Nancy J., & Schlick Noe, Katherine L. (1995). *Literature circles and response*. Norwood, MA: Christopher-Gordon Publishers, Inc.

Peterson, Ralph, & Eeds, Maryann. (1990). *Grand conversations: Literature groups in action*. New York: Scholastic.

Samway, Katharine Davies, & Whang, Gail. (1995). *Literature study circles in a multicultural classroom*. York, ME: Stenhouse.

Short, Kathy, & Pierce, Kathryn Mitchell (Eds.). (1990). *Talking about books: Creating literate communities*. Portsmouth, NH: Heinemann.

. . . on response to literature:

Holland, Kathleen, Hungerford, Rachael & Ernst, Shirley. (1993). *Journeying: Children responding to literature*. Portsmouth, NH: Heinemann.

Rief, Linda. (1999). *Vision & voice: Extending the literacy spectrum*. Portsmouth, NH: Heinemann.

Roser, Nancy L., & Martinez, Miriam G. (Eds.). (1995). *Book talk and beyond: Children and teachers respond to literature*. Newark, DE: International Reading Association.

. . . on assessment in literature circles:

Hill, Bonnie Campbell, & Ruptic, Cynthia. (1994). *Practical aspects of authentic assessment: Putting the pieces together*. Norwood, MA: Christopher-Gordon Publishers, Inc.

Hill, Bonnie Campbell, Ruptic, Cynthia, & Norwick, Lisa. (1998). *Classroom based assessment*. Norwood, MA: Christopher-Gordon Publishers, Inc.

And finally—what are the benefits all of this hard work? Janine King has that answer:

> It's simple, really. My students have gained an opportunity to enjoy books. They've been given a forum where they can do that. It includes such life-long tools—making their own choices, making their own decisions . . . the feeling of being trusted to be in charge of themselves. They've put it all together to come up with something meaningful.

Literature circles help you and your students "come up with something meaning-ful" together. Good luck . . . and get started!

—Katherine L. Schlick Noe and Nancy J. Johnson

References

Atwell, N. (1987). *In the middle: Reading, writing, and learning with adolescents* (p. 255). Portsmouth, NH: Heinemann.

Au, K. H., Carroll, J. A., & Shau, J. A. (1997). *Balanced literacy instruction.* Norwood, MA: Christopher-Gordon Publishers, Inc.

Avery, C. (1993). *And with a light touch: Learning about reading, writing and teaching with first graders.* Portsmouth, NH: Heinemann.

Bettelheim, B., & Zelan, K. (1981). *On learning to read: The child's fascination with meaning.* New York: Knopf, 306.

Brown, K. (1995). Going with the flow: Getting back on course when literature circles flounder. In B.C. Hill, N. J. Johnson, & K. L. Schlick Noe (Eds.), *Literature circles and response.* Norwood, MA: Christopher-Gordon Publishers, Inc.

Calkins, L. M. (1986). *The art of teaching writing.* Portsmouth, NH: Heinemann.

Clay, M. M. (1991). *Becoming literate: The construction of inner control* (p. 6). Portsmouth, NH: Heinemann.

Culham, R. (1998). *Picture books: An annotated bibliography with activities for teaching writing.* Portland, OR: Northwest Regional Educational Laboratory.

Daniels, H. (1994). *Literature circles: Voice and choice in the student-centered classroom.* York, ME: Steinhouse.

Fountas, I., & Pinnell, G. S. (1996). *Guided reading: Good first teaching for all students.* Portsmouth, NH: Heinemann.

Harris, V. J. (1997). *Using multiethnic literature in the K-8 classroom.* Norwood, MA: Christopher-Gordon Publishers, Inc.

Hill, B. C. (1995). Literature circles: Assessment and evaluation. In B. C. Hill, N. J. Johnson, & K. L. Schlick Noe. (Eds.), *Literature circles and response* (pp. 167–198). Norwood, MA: Christopher-Gordon Publishers, Inc.

Hill, B. C., Johnson, N. J., & Schlick Noe, K. L. (1995). *Literature circles and response.* Norwood, MA: Christopher-Gordon Publishers, Inc.

Hill, B. C. & Ruptic, C. (1994). *Practical aspects of authentic assessment: Putting the pieces together.* Norwood, MA: Christopher-Gordon Publishers, Inc.

Hill, B. C., Ruptic, C., & Norwick, L. (1998). *Classroom based assessment.* Norwood, MA: Christopher-Gordon Publishers, Inc.

Holland, K., Hungerford, R., & Ernst, S. (1993). *Journeying: Children responding to literature.* Portsmouth, NH: Heinemann.

The Horn Book. (1998). *The Horn Book guide, interactive.* Portsmouth, NH: Heinemann.

Huck, C. (1987). To know the place for the first time. *The best of the bulletin.* Children's Literature Assembly/National Council of Teachers of English, *1*, 69–71.

Kamber, P. (1995). Invisible scaffolding: Fostering reflection. In B.C. Hill, N. J. Johnson, & K. L. Schlick Noe. (Eds.). *Literature circles and response* (p. 102). Norwood, MA: Christopher-Gordon Publishers, Inc.

McClure, A., & Zitlow, C. (1991). Not just the facts: Aesthetic response in elementary content area studies. *Language Arts, 68,* 27–33.

Monson, D. (1995). Choosing books for literature circles. In B.C. Hill, N. J. Johnson, & K. L. Schlick Noe. (Eds.), *Literature circles and response* (p. 113). Norwood, MA: Christopher-Gordon Publishers, Inc.

Norwick, L. (1996). *Deepening response: Literature circles and the arts.* Presentation at the International Reading Association Annual Convention, New Orleans, Louisiana.

Ohlhausen, M. M., & Jepsen, M. (Winter 1992). Lessons from Goldilocks: Somebody's been choosing my books but I can make my own choices now! *The New Advocate, 5* (1), 36.

Owens, S. (1995). Treasures in the attic: Building the foundation for literature circles. In B.C. Hill, N .J. Johnson, & K. L. Schlick Noe (Eds.). *Literature circles and response* (pp. 1–12). Norwood, MA: Christopher-Gordon Publishers, Inc.

Paratore, J. R., & McCormack, R. L. (Eds.). (1997). *Peer talk in the classroom: Learning from research*. Newark, DE: International Reading Association.

Peterson, R., & Eeds, M. (1990). *Grand conversations* (p. 18). New York: Scholastic.

Peterson, R., & Eeds, M. (1991). Teacher as curator: Learning to talk about literature. *The Reading Teacher, 45*, 2, 125.

Rief, L. (1999). *Vision & voice: Extending the literacy spectrum*. Portsmouth, NH: Heinemann.

Rosenblatt, L. (1978). *The reader, the text, the poem: The transactive theory of the literary work*. Carbondale, IL: Southern Illinois Press.

Roser, N. L., & Martinez, M. G. (Eds.). *Book talk and beyond: Children and teachers respond to literature*. Newark, DE: International Reading Association.

Routman, R. (1991, 1994). *Invitations: Changing as teachers and learners K–12*. Portsmouth, NH: Heinemann.

Routman, R. (1996). *Literacy at the crossroads* (p. 49). Portsmouth, NH: Heinemann.

Samway, K. D., & Whang, G. (1996). *Literature study circles in a multicultural classroom*. York, ME: Stenhouse.

Short, K. G. (Ed.). (1995). *Research and professional resources in children's literature: Piecing a patchwork quilt*. Newark, DE: International Reading Association.

Short, K. G., & Pierce, K. M. (Eds.). (1990). *Talking about books: Creating literate communities*. Portsmouth, NH: Heinemann.

Sloan, M. (1995). *Literature circles and response: Inspiring genuine conversations*. Presentation at the International Reading Association Annual Convention, Anaheim, California.

Spiegel, D. L. (1998). Silver bullets, babies, and bath water: Literature response groups in a balanced literacy program. *The Reading Teacher, 52*, 2, 114–124.

Weaver, C. (1998). *Reconsidering a balanced approach to reading*. Urbana, IL: National Council of Teachers of English.

Children's Literature Cited

Avi. (1984). *The fighting ground*. New York: Lippincott.

Blume, Judy. (1981). *Freckle juice*. Illustrated by Sonia O. Lisker. New York: Four Winds Press.

Briggs, Raymond. (1970). *Jim and the beanstalk*. New York: Coward-McCann.

Bulla, Clyde Robert. (1987). *The chalk box kid*. Illustrated by Thomas B. Allen. New York: Random House.

Bunting, Eve. (1991). *Fly away home*. Illustrated by Ronald Himler. New York: Clarion.

Carlson, Natalie Savage. (1958). *Family under the bridge*. Pictures by Garth Williams. New York: Harper.

Catling, Patrick Skene. (1979). *The chocolate touch*. Pictures by Margot Apple. New York: Morrow.

Cherry, Lynne. (1990). *The great kapok tree*. San Diego: Harcourt Brace Jovanovich.

Cherry, Lynne. (1992). *A river ran wild*. San Diego: Harcourt Brace Jovanovich.

Cleary, Beverly. (1983). *Dear Mr. Henshaw*. Illustrated by Paul O. Zelinsky. New York: Morrow.

Collier, James Lincoln, & Collier, Christopher. (1974). *My brother Sam is dead*. New York: Simon & Schuster.

Curtis, Christopher Paul. (1995). *The Watsons go to Birmingham—1963*. New York: Delacorte.

Davidson, Margaret. (1988). *The story of Jackie Robinson: The bravest man in baseball*. Illustrated by Floyd Cooper. New York: Dell.

DeClements, Barthe. (1993). *The pickle song*. New York: Viking.

De Paola, Tomie. (1981). *Now one foot, now the other*. New York: Putnam.

Ehrlich, Amy. (reteller). (1985). *Cinderella*. Illustrated by Susan Jeffers. New York: Dial.

Fenner, Carol. (1991). *Randall's wall*. New York: M. K. McElderry Books.

Fleming, Denise. (1996). *Where once there was a wood*. New York: Henry Holt.

Forbes, Esther. (1943). *Johnny Tremain*. New York: Franklin Watts.

Fox, Mem. (1984). *Wilfrid Gordon McDonald Partridge*. Illustrated by Julie Vivas. Brooklyn, NY: Kane/Miller.

Fox, Paula. (1991). *Monkey Island*. New York: Greenwillow.

Gardiner, John Reynolds. (1980). *Stone Fox*. Illustrated by Marcia Sewell. New York: Crowell.

Garrigue, Sheila. (1985). *The eternal spring of Mr. Ito*. New York: Bradbury Press.

Gauch, Patricia. (1991). *Thunder at Gettysburg*. New York: Bantam.

George, Jean Craighead. (1995). *There's an owl in the shower*. Illustrated by Christine Herman Merrill. New York: HarperCollins.

George, Jean Craighead. (1988). *One day in the woods*. New York: Harper Trophy.

Henkes, Kevin. (1991). *Chrysanthemum*. New York: Greenwillow.

Hopkinson, Deborah. (1993). *Sweet Clara and the freedom quilt*. Illustrated by James Ransome. New York: Knopf.

Houston, Jean Wakatsuki. (1973). *Farewell to Manzanar*. New York: Bantam Books.

Howe, Deborah, & Howe, James. (1979). *Bunnicula*. Illustrated by Alan Daniel. New York: Atheneum.

Hughes, Dean. (1989). *Family pose*. New York: Atheneum.

Hurwitz, Johanna. (1979). *Aldo Applesauce*. Illustrated by John Wallner. New York: Morrow.

Hurwitz, Johanna. (1997). *Helen Keller: Courage in the dark*. Illustrated by Neverne Covington. New York: Random House.

Jackson, Ellen. (1994). *Cinder Edna*. Illustrated by Kevin O'Malley. New York: Lothrop, Lee & Shepard.

Johnston, Tony. (1985). *The quilt story*. Illustrated by Tomie De Paola. New York: Putnam.

Koller, Jackie French. (1995). *A place to call home*. New York: Atheneum.

Lauber, Patricia. (1988). *Lost star: The story of Amelia Earhart*. New York: Scholastic.

Lauber, Patricia. (1994). *Be a friend to trees*. Illustrated by Holly Keller. New York: HarperCollins.

Lewis, C. S. (1994). *The lion, the witch, and the wardrobe*. Illustrated by Pauline Baynes. New York: Harper.

Lobel, Arnold. (1979). *Frog and Toad together*. New York: Harper Trophy.

Magorian, Michelle. (1981). *Good Night, Mr. Tom*. New York: Harper & Row.

Marshall, James. (1973). *Yummers!* Boston: Houghton Mifflin.

Marshall, James. (1986). *Three up a tree*. New York: Dial.

Marshall, James. (1986). *Yummers too!* Boston: Houghton Mifflin.

McKissack, Patricia C., & McKissack, Fredrick. (1988). *Sojourner Truth: Ain't I a woman?* New York: Scholastic.

McPhail, David. (reteller). (1995). *Little Red Riding Hood.* New York: Scholastic.

McSwigan, Marie. (1942). *Snow treasure.* Illustrated by Mary Reardon. New York: Dutton.

Means, Florence Crannell. (1992). *The moved-outers.* New York: Walker.

Mitchell, Margaree King. (1993). *Uncle Jed's barbershop.* Illustrated by James Ransome. New York: Simon & Schuster.

Myers, Walter Dean. (1988). *Scorpions.* New York: Harper & Row.

Myers, Walter Dean. (1992). *Somewhere in the darkness.* New York: Scholastic.

Myers, Walter Dean. (1993). *Malcolm X: By any means necessary.* New York: Scholastic.

Myers, Walter Dean. (1994). *The glory field.* New York: Scholastic.

Myers, Walter Dean. (1996). *Slam!* New York: Scholastic.

Naidoo, Beverly. (1985). *Journey to Jo'burg: A South African story.* Illustrated by Eric Velasquez. New York: J. B. Lippincott.

Naylor, Phyllis Reynolds. (1991). *Shiloh.* New York: Dell.

O'Dell, Scott. (1980). *Sarah Bishop.* Boston: Houghton Mifflin.

Parish, Peggy. (1963). *Amelia Bedelia.* Pictures by Fritz Siebel. New York: Harper & Row.

Park, Barbara. (1987). *The kid in the red jacket.* New York: Knopf.

Paterson, Katherine. (1978). *The Great Gilly Hopkins.* New York: Crowell.

Perlman, Janet. (1993). *Cinderella Penguin, or, the little glass flipper.* New York: Viking.

Perlman, Janet. (1995). *Emperor Penguin's new clothes.* New York: Viking.

Polacco, Patricia. (1990). *Babushka's doll.* New York: Simon & Schuster.

Polacco, Patricia. (1990). *Thunder cake.* New York: Philomel.

Rand, Gloria. (1992). *Prince William.* Illustrated by Ted Rand. New York: Henry Holt.

Rathmann, Peggy. (1991). *Ruby the copycat.* New York: Scholastic.

Rathmann, Peggy. (1995). *Officer Buckle and Gloria.* New York: Putnam.

Rosen, Michael J. (Ed.). (1992). *Home: A collaboration of thirty distinguished authors and illustrators of children's books to aid the homeless.* New York: HarperCollins.

Rylant, Cynthia. (1987). *Henry and Mudge: The first book of their adventures.* Pictures by Sucie Stevenson. New York: Bradbury Press.

Sachar, Louis. (1987). *There's a boy in the girls' bathroom.* New York: Knopf.

Schroeder, Alan. (1996). *Satchmo's blues.* Illustrated by Floyd Cooper. New York: Doubleday.

Scieszka, Jon. (1989). *The true story of the three pigs.* Illustrated by Lane Smith. New York: Viking.

Scieszka, Jon. (1991). *The Frog Prince continued.* Illustrated by Lane Smith. New York: Trumpet.

Sharmat, Marjorie Weinman. (1972). *Nate the Great.* Illustrated by Marc Simont. New York: Coward-McCann.

Sharpe, Susan. (1990). *Waterman's boy.* New York: Bradbury Press.

Sperry, Armstrong. (1940). *Call it courage.* New York: Macmillan.

Spinelli, Jerry. (1990). *Maniac Magee.* Boston: Little, Brown.

Taylor, Mildred. (1976). *Roll of thunder, hear my cry.* New York: Dial.

Taylor, Mildred. (1981). *Let the circle be unbroken.* New York: Dial.

Thesman, Jean. (1992). *When the road ends.* New York: Avon.

Uchida, Yoshiko. (1971). *Journey to Topaz.* Illustrated by Donald Carrick. New York: Scribner's Sons.

Uchida, Yoshiko. (1992). *The invisible thread.* New York: Messner.

Uchida, Yoshiko. (1993). *The bracelet.* Illustrated by Joanna Yardley. New York: Philomel.

Voigt, Cynthia. (1981). *Homecoming.* New York: Atheneum.

Warner, Gertrude Chandler. (1942). *The boxcar children.* Illustrated by L. Kate Deal. Chicago: A. Whitman.

White, E. B. (1945). *Stuart Little.* Pictures by Garth Williams. New York: Harper & Row.

White, E. B. (1952). *Charlotte's web.* Pictures by Garth Williams. New York: Harper & Row.

White, E. B. (1970). *Trumpet of the swan.* Pictures by Edward Frascino. New York: Puffin.

Williams, Vera B. (1982). *A chair for my mother.* New York: Greenwillow.

Woodruff, Elvira. (1991). *George Washington's socks.* New York: Scholastic.

Index

A

Assessment, 12
   See also Discussion, Focus lessons, Extension projects, Response journals

B

Beginning readers and writers, 17, 18, 70, 78
Book talks, 15, 23, 29
Books for literature circles, 35-40
   book sets, 38-40
   criteria, 35
   for a range of abilities and interests, 38
   guiding student selection, 16
   multiple copies, 38
   resources for, 37
   to begin with, 36-37
   See also Structure

C

Challenged readers, 7, 18, 29-30, 38, 61
Classroom climate, 7-10
   collaboration and respect, 7-8
   independence and responsibility, 8-9, 32, 33
   response to literature, 9-10
Common questions
   books, 40
   classroom climate, 10
   discussion, 59-62
   extension projects, 105-106
   focus lessons, 89
   response journals, 76-79
   structure, 32-34

D

Discussion, 41-62
   and response journals, 46, 55
   assessment, 56-58
     anecdotal notes, 56-57
     checklists, 57
     rubrics, 58
     student self-reflection, 57-58
   debriefing, 12, 29, 31, 42, 51, 55, 56, 60, 61

formats and structure, 18-21, 25-26, 30-31, 43
fostering quality, 59
framework for discussion, 43-56
   what to talk about, 44-47
   gathering information to share, 47-50
   learning to participate in discussion, 51-56
   self-reflection, 55-56
goals, 42
making discussions work, 42
roles
   of other adults, 59
   of students, 18-21, 30-31, 60
   of the teacher, 26, 30
schedule and length, 23, 25, 29, 33, 59
teaching, 51-55
   brainstorming, 51
   developing guidelines, 52-53
   discussion etiquette, 52-53
   practice and debrief, 55
tools
   bookmarks, 48
   Golden Lines, 48, 49
   guided topic, 45
   open invitation, 44
   Post-it Notes, 24, 34, 47, 62
   prompts, 45
   quote and question, 44
   discussion logs, 48-50
   student-generated questions, 46-47
troubleshooting, 60-61
See also Structure

E

Extension projects, 91-106
   and book reports, 92
   and rereading, 93, 105
   assessment, 102-105
     checklists, 103
     presentations, 103-105
     student self-reflection, 102-103
   definition and benefits, 91-92

examples, 92-94
    ABC Book, 94
    Accordion Book, 93
    CD Cover, 94
    Character Bookmark, 93, 96-98
    Commemorative Stamp, 94
    Jackdaw, 94
    Story Hat, 27, 93
    Story Quilt, 94, 97-101
fostering quality, 106
management, 106
presentations, 101-102
teaching process, 94-101
See also Structure

F

Focus lessons, 81-89
    components, 86-87
    definition, 81
    management, 87-88
    teaching, 25
    types of 82-86
        literature circle procedures, 83
        literature qualities, 85-86
        reading, writing, and response
            strategies, 83-85
Forms and handouts
    discussion
        Bookmark, 48
        Discussion Etiquette, 53
        Discussion Evaluation Form, 56
        Discussion Log, 49
        Discussion Rating Form, 58
        Literature Response Log, 50
    focus lessons
        Focus Lessons Checklist, 88
    extension projects
        Book Presentation Evaluation, 104
        Story Quilt Assignment (older
            readers), 100
        Story Quilt Assignment (younger
            readers), 99
        Student and Teacher Evaluation
            Form, 104
    response journals
        Journal Prompts, 66
        Rubric for Journal Responses, 75
    use of, 33, 50

L

Literature circles
    in a balanced reading program, 1-2
    benefits for students, 2

definition, ix
key questions, xi, xii
research base, ix
setting goals and teaching to them, 3-5
underlying assumptions, x-xi
working with families, 33-34

M

Modeling and demonstration
    book selection, 24
    discussion, 18, 19, 20, 26, 33, 42, 44, 45, 48, 54
    during read aloud, 9-10
    extension projects, 12, 95, 96, 97, 98, 100
    focus lessons, 81-82, 86
    response journals, 63, 67, 71, 72-74, 77, 79

P

Published literature guides, 68, 78, 82

R

Reading, *See* Challenged readers and writers, Discussion, Focus lessons, Response journals, Structure
Resources
    books, 38-40
    professional books, 37
    professional journals, 37
    web sites and computer resources, 37-38
    See also Books for literature circles
Response journals, 63-79
    and discussion, 46, 55, 77, 78
    assessment, 74-76
        rubrics, 74-75
        student self-reflection, 75
    format, 26, 31, 76-77
    fostering quality, 77
    growth over time, 71-72
    making journals work, 63
    management, 12
    prompts, 65-67
    purpose, 64-65
    time for journals, 23, 29, 78
    teaching, 72-74
    troubleshooting, 77
    types of journal entries, 68-71
        cause/effect, 69
        character web, 70
        diary, 68

letters, 69
sketches and drawings, 70-71
questions
    from discussion, 67-68
    from outside resources, 68
responding to students writing, 78-79
See also Structure

S

Structure, 11-34
    choosing books and forming groups,
        15-17, 29
    discussion, 18-21, 25-26, 30-31
    examples
        first grade, 12, 22-27
        fourth grade, 12, 27-32
        sixth grade, 12
    extension projects, 21, 27, 31
    Literacy Block fourth grade, 29

management, 21-22
planning, 11-15
reading literature circle books, 17-18,
    24, 29-30
Reading/Writing Workshop first
    grade, 23
schedules
    weekly, 23, 28-29
    yearly, 13, 28
written response, 21, 26, 31
See also Discussion, Response jour-
    nals, Extension projects

V

Vocabulary, 49, 89

W

Writing, *See* Challenged readers and writers, Discussion, Focus lessons, Response
journals, Structure

About the Authors

Katherine L. Schlick Noe is Associate Professor and Coordinator of Reading at Seattle University. A former high school teacher, she received her Ph.D. in Reading/Language Arts from the University of Washington. She is also coeditor, with Bonnie Campbell Hill and Nancy J. Johnson, of *Literature Circles and Response,* also published by Christopher-Gordon.

Nancy J. Johnson is an Associate Professor at Western Washington University. Prior to receiving her Ph.D. from Michigan State University, she taught both 5th and 9th grades. She is coeditor, with Bonnie Campbell Hill and Katherine Schlick Noe, of *Literature Circles and Response,* also published by Christopher-Gordon.